Developing PORTFOLIOS in EDUCATION

Developing PORTFOLIOS in EDUCATION

A Guide to Reflection, Inquiry, and Assessment

Ruth S. Johnson
J. Sabrina Mims-Cox
Adelaide Doyle-Nichols
California State University, Los Angeles

SAGE Publications
Thousand Oaks ▪ London ▪ New Delhi

For information:

Sage Publications, Inc.
2455 Teller Road
Thousand Oaks, California 91320
E-mail: order@sagepub.com

Sage Publications Ltd.
1 Oliver's Yard
55 City Road
London EC1Y 1SP
United Kingdom

Sage Publications India Pvt. Ltd.
B-42, Panchsheel Enclave
Post Box 4109
New Delhi 110 017 India

Printed in the United States of America.

Library of Congress Cataloging-in-Publication Data

Johnson, Ruth S.
Developing portfolios in education : a guide to reflection, inquiry,
and assessment / Ruth S. Johnson, J. Sabrina Mims-Cox, Adelaide Doyle-Nichols.
p. cm.
Includes bibliographical references and index.
ISBN 1-4129-1389-6 (pbk.)
1. Portfolios in education—United States. 2. Portfolios in education—
United States—Evaluation. 3. Teachers—Rating of—United States.
4. Teachers—Training of—United States. I. Mims-Cox, J. Sabrina.
II. Doyle-Nichols, Adelaide. III. Title.
LB1029.P67J656 2006
370'.71'1—dc22

2005023104

This book is printed on acid-free paper.

06 07 08 09 10 11 9 8 7 6 5 4 3 2 1

Acquisitions Editor: Diane McDaniel
Associate Editor: Margo Beth Crouppen
Editorial Assistant: Erica Carroll
Project Editor: Tracy Alpern
Copy Editor: Angela Buckley
Typesetter: C&M Digitals (P) Ltd.
Indexer: Pamela Van Huss
Cover Designer: Michelle Kenny

Contents

CD Contents

Acknowledgments

Many people helped us in shaping the contents, format, and organization of this book. Their guidance, time, and emotional support were invaluable.

Our current and former students and colleagues at California State University, Los Angeles, inspired much of the work in this book. Professors Ann Hafner, John Schindler, and Fawn Ukpolo contributed research, instructional, and assessment documents. John Schindler also opened his classroom and generously allowed for taping of portfolio presentations. The Curriculum and Instruction Directed Teaching Committee members, Kimberly Persiani-Becker, Dolores Beltran, Andrea Maxie, Rebecca Joseph, Rosario Morales, and Sabrina Mims-Cox, developed and provided draft portfolio rubric samples for the final multiple subject and single subject portfolio presentation sessions. These draft rubrics guided much of our work for rubrics in Chapters 4, 5, and 6 in terms of portfolio organization, contents, and evaluation. We are especially grateful for the materials and guidance that C. D. and Sharon Johnson shared with us based on their extensive work with "Results Based" portfolios for counselors. We also appreciate Kathy Reilly's contribution in the counseling area. Samples of student work, photos, and portfolio presentations for the CD were contributed by the following teacher and administrator candidates: Kisha Griggs, Bernice Suen, Kathleen Perez, Brooke Schufreider, Alicia Stanco, Judy Peng, Helen Simmons Conroy, Matthew Ginsberg, Stephanie Frederick, Yasmin Martinez, Alma Moran, Josefina Zacarias-Ayala, Karin Aguilar, Brenda Sanchez, Soon-Ya Chang, Karen Gilmartin, Ysenia Mancilla, Antonio Cova, Sylvia Torres, Leticia Orozco, Pamela Perkins, Jean Ammon, Kirk Nichols, Rosa Paredes, Violet Medina Bartolini, Laura Pérez-Vásquez, John Glaister, María Sandoval, and Lesly Lespinasse (teacher candidates); and Adrienne Balcazar, Hedy Bravo-Juarez, Gudiel Croswaite, Constantino Duarte, James Eder, Stephan Franklin, Flavio Gallarzo, Myriam Islas, Trish Luckeroth Lockhart, Brenda Loh, Karen D. Magana, Lusine Martinzyan, Ambler

Moss, Hipolito Murillo, Margaret Olivares-Gilkyson, Consuelo M. Rodriguez-Garcia, Greg Runyon, Dinorah Sanchez, Luis Sanchez, and Odell Scott (administrator candidates).

We thank Beth Cornell, Director of Fine Arts and Humanities from the Pennsylvania Department of Education, Division of Evaluation and Reports, for her consultation and guidance in the use of the Portfolio Implementation Guide (Pennsylvania Assessment Through Themes, PATT). We also appreciate the advice and assistance from Kirk Nichols, who reviewed parts of the manuscript and helped out with videotaping for the CD and other technical matters, and from Ann West, who read our manuscript and provided us with insightful and useful editorial comments. We thank Shirley Blueford and Wendy Lue for their assistance and inspiration during the long meetings and writing.

Our families and significant others had to delay together times and provide support for us during our writing journey. Adelaide would like to thank Kirk and Stephanie for their love, understanding, and support. She would also like to thank Stephen and Adelaide for their guidance and for instilling in her a desire to achieve. J. Sabrina would like to thank her mother, Willie Mae Mims, and her husband, Woodrow Cox, for their love, patience, and support throughout this process. She would also like to thank her siblings, Wayne, Wyatt, Willis, and Salimu, for their constant encouragement. Ruth would like to thank her daughters, Shawn Johnson-Witt and Cathy Payne, for their patience, love, and support and her grandchildren, Glenn and Shawn II, who serve as an inspiration and motivation to improve the educational enterprise.

Our Sage acquisitions editor, Diane McDaniel, has provided us with guidance and support. She has been patient and understanding when work was delayed. We thank her deeply. Sage Associate Editor Margo Beth Crouppen also assisted us in the development of the CD that accompanies this book. Her assistance was appreciated. We would also like to thank the peer reviewers who aided us in shaping the text so that it would best serve our readers:

Carrie E. Chapman, Indiana University
Kimberly Kinsler, Hunter College of the City University of New York
Ann M. Rule, Saint Louis University
Shawn J. Witt, University of La Verne
Kevin S. Sherman, Auburn University
Patricia A. Parrish, Saint Leo University
Natalie B. Milman, The George Washington University

Introduction for Instructors

As instructors in higher education we realized that using portfolios with our students was increasingly transforming the way in which we interacted with and engaged them in the learning process. Infusing reflective practice and designing fundamentally different ways to evaluate work required changes in practice. We sought out resources to assist us and found that there was a large body of print and electronic materials on various aspects of portfolio development, assessment, and evaluation. However, we felt the need for a comprehensive text that would serve as a resource throughout a professional's career.

We began our work by shaping a text with a focus on faculty and students who were at the beginning stages of instituting portfolios for assessment and evaluation of candidates. Our purpose for faculty was to develop a text that would be useful for both candidates and instructors—one that would provide a conceptual and research framework about the usefulness of portfolios, suggest some ways to organize the process, and provide long-term, useful tools that would be used at various stages of a professional's career, including professional and academic advancement. A central feature that we wanted to incorporate was a chapter on the electronic portfolio. Some highlights of the electronic features that accompany this book include a CD for instructors with guidelines, PowerPoint presentations, Web- and hyperlinks, portfolio models and templates, implementation guidelines, and research bases. These are indicated in the text by a CD icon.

Introduction for Students

Portfolios have fast become a desired tool for assessing students because they provide authentic evidence of what students know, believe, and are able to do. While working with our own students in their various credential programs, we, as authors, soon realized that a common element of each credential program in our university was the portfolio requirement. We also realized that there was not a clear and consistent format given to students in preparing their portfolios, or to faculty on how to assist their students in the portfolio process. The purpose of this book is to provide direct support to students as they complete their portfolios in partial fulfillment of their credential or other degree programs. A primary goal of this book is to clearly describe how portfolios are defined, organized, and evaluated so that students will have concrete examples of what is expected of them throughout the portfolio process. A second goal is to assist students in retooling the portfolio for reflection and professional development beyond the credential program.

We began our work by shaping a text with a focus on students who were at the beginning stages of their credential or degree program, when portfolios were used for assessment and evaluation of candidates. We wanted to develop a text that would be useful for both candidates and instructors—one that would provide a conceptual and research framework about the usefulness of portfolios, but also to suggest some practical ways to organize the process and to provide long-term, useful tools that would be used during programs and for professional and academic advancement beyond a specific program. A central feature that we wanted to include was a chapter on the electronic portfolio. Some highlights of the electronic features that accompany the book include a CD with guidelines, PowerPoint presentations, Web- and hyperlinks, portfolio models and templates, implementation guidelines, and research bases. These are indicated in the text by a CD icon.

PART I

The Rationale for Developing Portfolios

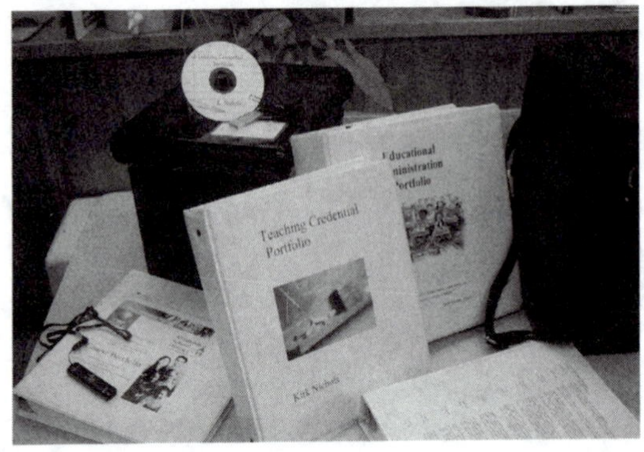

1

Why Develop a Portfolio?

The development of portfolios by students has been lauded by teachers and principals as especially useful in graphically portraying academic and creative abilities and in enhancing learning.

—Brown and Irby (2001)

Chapter Objectives

Readers will be able to

- describe the current trends and uses of portfolios in kindergarten through postsecondary education,
- describe a portfolio and its purposes,
- explain the need for documents that authentically assess learning outcomes for aspiring and practicing educators,
- discuss some of the benefits and challenges of portfolio development.

Scenario

The College of Education at Sunshine University recently instituted the requirement of portfolio assessment for evaluating competency in professional standards of their teacher, administrative, and school counselor candidates. The college is scheduled in the next academic year for a visitation from state and national accrediting agencies. There is some anxiety and concern about how the college will perform. The state accreditation agency requires multiple assessments for candidate certification, and the portfolio is one of the required assessments. Some professors in teacher education programs are familiar with portfolio use and have instructed their teacher credential candidates in their methodology courses on how to develop portfolios for their pre-K–12 students. However, they are uncertain about how to implement this type of assessment in their own college classes and programs. The educational administration and school counseling programs use only comprehensive exams to determine competency for graduation.

Most of the instructors are dissatisfied with current assessments, but until now, they had no impetus to change. The accreditation requirements presented an opportunity to implement a change that would have the potential to improve the preparation and assessment of aspiring educational candidates.

In class discussions about portfolios, many inconsistencies surfaced in the ways that instructors described a portfolio, the portfolio's purpose, portfolio organization, and how the portfolios would be evaluated. Many of the syllabi and classes did an inadequate job of addressing the required standards. Moreover, there were major inconsistencies in how performance was measured, the quality and quantity of work expected, and the levels of rigor required to demonstrate competency. As the college began the process of portfolio implementation, instructors and students realized that portfolio development is a complex process that requires study and evaluation. Overall, the college and its students were willing to embrace the process because portfolio development and assessment were viewed as good opportunities for demonstration of how students and the college performed on important professional standards.

Overview

The above scenario describes some of the expectations and dilemmas in using portfolios to assess the competency in meeting professional standards of candidates in schools, agencies, and colleges of education. Professional educators are now teaching in an era of standards-based reforms. Forty-nine states have adopted standards for a variety of subjects at K–12 levels of education. There is mounting evidence that clear goals, high standards, and high expectations contribute to improved student performance.

Similarly, the standards movement is having a profound effect on colleges and schools in higher education. States are rapidly requiring that preparation and credential programs meet national and/or state standards and that candidates be assessed for competency in meeting those standards. Portfolios are being selected as a major way to measure those competencies. According to Georgi and Crowe (1998), portfolios are commonplace in today's schools and universities. Likewise, Salzman, Denner, and Harris (2002, in Wilkerson & Lang, 2003) report that nearly 90 percent of schools, colleges, and departments of education use portfolios in evaluating their candidates and about 40 percent use portfolios in certification or licensure requirement. Portfolios are also emerging as a component of career advancement and professional evaluation in schools and districts (Brown & Irby, 2000; Campbell et al., 2001; National Board for Professional Teaching Standards, 1999). The National Board for Professional Teaching Standards (NBPTS) requires the submission of portfolios as a major component in determining National Board Certified Teachers. These current demands place portfolios in an important role in pre-K–12 schools and colleges of education.

Until recently, portfolios in higher education were used primarily in preservice teacher education programs (Bartell, Kaye, & Morin, 1998; Campbell et al., 2001; Campbell, Melenyzer, Nettles, & Wyman, 2000, 2004; Stone, 1998) but to a lesser extent in leadership and other preparation programs, such as school counseling (Barnes, Clark, & Thull, 2005; Barnett, 1992; Brown & Irby, 2000, 2001). There is extensive literature to inform and shape our knowledge of portfolio use, portfolio contents, and portfolio development, but there is limited information about institutional issues related to portfolio development and evaluation (Meadows & Dyal, 1999; Wilkerson & Lang, 2003; Wyatt & Looper, 1999). The remainder of this chapter describes portfolios and their use as assessment and evaluation tools, and the benefits and challenges of portfolio use. The chapter concludes with a summary and an introduction to the chapters that follow.

What Is a Portfolio?

Initially, a portfolio may appear as simply a collection of work that has been compiled over a period of time. Portfolios are sometimes compared with scrapbooks. Although both may contain artifacts that are selected over time, portfolio contents are organized to assess competencies in a given standard, goal, or objective and focus on how well the learner achieves in that area. Through the use of *artifacts,* which are concrete examples of the candidate's work, *portfolios* contain evidence of knowledge, dispositions, and skills (Brown & Irby, 2001). A portfolio that is used for assessment and evaluation requires a candidate to engage in higher levels of thinking through the use of inquiry and reflection. *Inquiry* involves a process of collecting, sorting, selecting, describing, analyzing, and evaluating evidence to answer questions on how well the evidence represents the candidate's accomplishment of a standard, goal, or objective. The candidate is involved in a personal type of action research that entails continual *reflection* or questioning and resorting of the selected work. The candidate is also questioning how he or she must improve personal practice. This process is described more fully in Chapters 2 and 3.

Purposes for Portfolios

Portfolios serve a variety of purposes. For example, they are used as assessment instruments, to display outstanding work, and to measure levels of competency for certification, graduation requirements, and career advancement. Barton and Collins (1997) highlighted the fact that portfolios are

- Another method to evaluate the success of a graduate
- A way to give candidates and faculty the opportunity to reflect on candidate progress
- A method to translate the learning from instructors to candidates
- A way to allow instructors to evaluate a variety of specific evidence when making global determinations about learner competency

The purpose for which the portfolio is designed should determine its organization, content, and presentation style. There are a variety of portfolio styles, each with a specific purpose. Table 1.1, although not exhaustive, presents information about the features of different kinds of portfolios. Some types have similar or overlapping uses, or both.

Using Portfolios for Assessment and Evaluation

One might ask, What are the incentives to use portfolios for assessment and evaluation? When portfolios are described as an assessment tool for individuals, programs, and institutions, *assessment* is defined as an ongoing, developmental process to measure growth and change and that provides information on areas that need further development. *Evaluation* usually describes a final, summative process that includes multiple assessments and is akin to a high-stakes test or a recommendation for credentials, promotion, or graduation (Landau & Bogus, 1975; Morris, 1976). These topics are described more fully in Chapter 2.

Table 1.1 Types of Portfolios

Type	*Purpose*	*Unique Features*	*Use*
1. Academic (Brown & Irby, 2001) and Educational Assessment (Wyatt & Looper, 1999; Bartell, Kaye, & Morin, 1998)	For assessment and evaluation of candidates and in-program evaluation	Contains artifacts and reflections based on academic classes, projects, field experiences, and/or programs	To show academic and experiential growth for credentials, certification, and graduation
2. Career Advancement and Employment (Brown & Irby, 2001; Bartell, Kaye, & Morin, 1998; Satterthwaite & D'Orsi, 2003)	Provides information on experiences that are relevant to professional advancement	Contains evidence of career accomplishments	For employment interviews, professional advancement, and follow-up after interviews
3. Learning and Teaching (Bartell, Kaye, & Morin, 1998)	Promotes candidate's reflection and ownership of the learning process	Personalized collections of a candidate's work, emphasizing ownership and self-assessment	For exploring, extending, showcasing, and reflecting on personal learning
4. Developmental (Wyatt & Looper, 1999)	Shows the stages of growth and development of the individual over time	An individual selects work that demonstrates sequential development over time. It is reflective of growth over time	An evaluation of the candidate's developmental work
5. Showcase (Wyatt & Looper, 1999)	A showcase to demonstrate achievement and to impress others	Is dynamic, showcases the best work to demonstrate a competency, and is kept current	For presentation to an audience (e.g., professor, employer, evaluator)

Type	*Purpose*	*Unique Features*	*Use*
6. Presentation (Campbell et al., 2001)	An easy-to-read display of competence	Samples of the best work from a portfolio collection	For presentations to an audience
7. Working (Campbell et al., 2001)	Shows professional growth	An ongoing, systematic collection of work over time	A self-assessment and goal-setting tool
8. Comprehensive (Johnson, Mims-Cox, & Doyle-Nichols, 2006)	A storehouse for keeping a myriad of artifacts that will be used for career and academic advancement	Up-to-date resource file with organizational features	Used to select specific artifacts to develop different types of *focus portfolios* (see Chapter 8)
9. Focus (Johnson, Mims-Cox, & Doyle-Nichols, 2006)	For presentation in academic and career advancement settings	Focused on a specific area related to academic and career advancement	For preparation and presentation in job or in higher-education interview; self- and supervisor evaluation; analysis of strengths and weaknesses for planning professional development (see Chapter 8)

There is ample literature supporting the notion that a collection of well-organized, real-world concrete artifacts in a portfolio offers the potential to assess in powerful ways how a student or candidate has developed and how a candidate applied what was learned (Barton & Collins, 1997; Sewell, Marczak, & Horn, 2005; Shaklee, Barbour, Ambrose, & Hansford, 1997). Portfolios have been viewed, historically, as one of the most comprehensive and effective forms of authentic assessment since the late 1980s (Barton & Collins,

1997; Sewell et al., 2005; Shaklee et al., 1997), because they provide a systematic way of organizing and documenting real-life evidence of a person's performance.

For many years, portfolios have been used to demonstrate competencies in areas such as architecture, art, and the performance fields, in which concrete demonstrations of competencies are critical. The contents of portfolios include multiple ways to assess complex knowledge and problem-solving skills. Instruments such as videos, graphics, audios, field documents, and other concrete information can be used to demonstrate competency toward standards.

Moreover, portfolios need not be the sole assessment tool. We advocate that they serve as enhancements to more traditional academic models, such as comprehensive exams, field observations by supervisors, and licensure exams. Portfolios provide alternative ways for candidates to demonstrate and document their level of achievement and competency toward meeting or exceeding a standard, goal, or objective (Barton & Collins, 1997, Pennsylvania Assessment Through Themes, 2000; Sewell et al., 2005; Shaklee et al., 1997). See Chapter 2 for a more robust discussion of this topic, including examples of how artifacts are transformed into evidence.

Benefits of Portfolios

The development of a portfolio encourages learners to shift from playing a passive role in assessment and evaluation—in which they are pressed to focus on external issues, such as what questions the instructors are going to ask and what they should be studying—to an active role, in which they must engage in more complex thinking and self-evaluation in choosing representations of what they learned. This route thus requires candidates to reflect on and demonstrate their competencies with real-world artifacts.

The development of a portfolio ideally evolves as a dynamic interaction among instructors, learners, and mentors. This interaction fosters a more interpersonal approach to teaching and learning, an approach that is responsive to all students, but particularly to African American, Hispanic, and Native American students (Irvine, 1990; Ladson-Billings, 1994). Portfolios also offer another way of measuring competencies for those who do not score well on traditional exams (Astin, 1993; Dollase, 1996; Steele, 2002). The process also can encourage peer evaluation whereby candidates collaborate with and assist each other in selecting artifacts, critiquing the evidence, organizing the portfolio, and providing general support.

Portfolios offer the opportunity to assess competencies in how effectively educational candidates are responding to diverse student groups.

Our nation is experiencing demographics shifts, and these changes are reflected in our public school enrollments. Many states have high percentages of students with a primary language other than English. Other pertinent factors involve the cultural, environmental, and economic contexts in which educators, students, and families interact. The National Commission on Teaching and America's Future report "What Matters Most: Teaching for America's Future" (1996) argues that teacher content knowledge and pedagogical strategies have a powerful effect on student achievement, particularly for students in low-achieving, low-income urban and rural schools.

Many of the INTASC (Interstate New Teachers Assessment and Support Consortium) Principles, such as Principle 3, "Adapting Instructions for Individual Needs"; Principle 5, "Classroom Motivation and Management"; Principle 7, Instructional Planning Skills; and Principle 8, Assessment of Student Learning, are principles that should be measured in ways that demonstrate how knowledge is transformed to practice to meet the needs of diverse student groups. Indicators of *dispositions,* which reflect beliefs, values, and expectations for diverse groups of children, are critical areas to assess. Richer sources of evidence can be required and provided through the effective use of case studies, videos, lesson plans and instructional strategies, observations of student and parent interactions, and student responses and reflection on lessons, to name a few. A body of work is emerging in the area of culturally responsive classrooms and schools that can serve as a resource in this area. (Johnson, 2002; Johnson & Bush, 2005; Ladson-Billings, 1994; Lee, 1997; Lindsey, Robins, & Terrell, 2005; Robins, Lindsey, Lindsey, & Terrell, 2002; Shade, Kelly, & Oberg, 2004).

At the program and institutional levels, the potential for feedback and professional improvement is immense. Candidates' reflections, when made part of the portfolio development process, provide assessment information about what was learned in courses and about program strengths, weaknesses, and levels of implementation. Because each candidate's voice can be heard during portfolio presentations and reviews of written documentation, program instructors, mentors, and supervisors may gain valuable insights about the efficacy of their instruction and programs. When programs and schools use information from the portfolios as a component of continuous evaluation, candidates' achievements become the focus of curriculum and strategies. Reflection can provide program developers with vital information about how well learners have integrated the values, knowledge, and meaning from their instruction and mentoring (see video clips for Chapter 6, Presenting the Portfolio).

Challenges in Portfolio Development

Major institutional challenges to portfolio development include time, resources, commitment, and the design and implementation of agreed-upon rubrics for scoring work. The portfolio process is labor intensive compared to scoring a multiple-choice exam. Although individual instructors may have embraced the use of portfolios, most institutional structures, climates, and processes are poor hosts for portfolio development. When ineffective institutional implementation practices exist, they diminish the effectiveness of portfolios as methods for assessment and evaluation.

A former candidate described how poor institutional practices affected him:

> I have begun in earnest to review the stack of documents and artifacts that will comprise my portfolio and I have a few concerns. Mostly, I feel confused because so much of the jargon and other stuff [is] new to me. It's not clear to me that my course work prepared me specifically for this particular task. (To this end, . . . I would like to suggest that the department make the portfolio an integral part of each class, rather than a separate component to be assembled at the end of all course work.) Were it not for my being a pack rat, I probably would not have kept any of my "old work," since no one prompted me to do so. (Candidate Reflection)

Wilkerson and Lang (2003) offer compelling arguments about the need to understand the psychometric implications of portfolio assessments, particularly if these are used to make decisions about a candidate's credential, licensure, and/or graduation. In our view, such arguments should be heeded. If not, issues of whether portfolio assessments can be considered a worthy measure of a candidate's professional competency are liable to come under question at some point, thus potentially undermining the credibility of programs and evaluation. Such issues will be more fully presented in Chapter 3.

To meet these challenges, the following guidelines for institutional practice might be considered:

1. Develop clear goals, outcomes, and timelines related to process and candidate achievement.
2. Review the literature on effective practices. Revise content and approaches to teaching and learning.
3. Establish guidelines for the nature of discourse that is desired among instructors, candidates, and mentors.
4. If needed, revise department structures to enhance the facilitation of portfolio development.

5. Design courses to align coherently with the portfolio development process.
6. Press for the allocation and reallocation of resources for professional development in the area of assessment and evaluation related to portfolios (see Chapters 2 and 4).
7. Encourage stakeholders with a vested interest in the quality of candidates to communicate, collaborate, and critique the assessment process.
8. Provide guidelines for program instructors to give ongoing appropriate direction, advisement, and support to candidates in the development of the portfolio and its retooling for future use.
9. Create a system to monitor and evaluate "implementation fidelity" (see Chapter 4).

Summary

Portfolios are becoming a popular method for assessment and evaluation of candidates in schools and colleges of education. In some institutions, portfolios are used along with other assessment measures, but in other institutions, they may be the sole criterion for judging competency. Many external agencies, such as state credentialing agencies, currently require portfolio assessment.

Portfolios can provide evidence of knowledge, dispositions, and skills. A large body of information maintains that well-organized, reflective portfolios can offer authentic information about how a candidate has progressed and at what levels of competency a candidate has achieved. Portfolios can be used for a variety of purposes, including showcasing work, measuring competency, establishing certification and graduation requirements, and pursuing career advancement. Although we know of many benefits of portfolio use, there are also some challenges. To meet the challenge of being accepted as authentic assessments for candidate evaluation, portfolios will need to be developed in institutions where they are carefully designed, implemented, monitored, and evaluated. The following topics pertaining to portfolio development and implementation are presented in the remaining chapters:

Chapter 2: Using portfolios as tools for authentic assessment and evaluation

Chapter 3: Describing the importance of portfolios as an element of reflective practice

Chapter 4: Organizing and implementing the portfolio as a developmental process

Chapter 5: Providing a guide for portfolio content and templates and suggesting ways to select artifacts to demonstrate competencies

Chapter 6: Describing ways to present a portfolio and presenting other practical applications of portfolios

Chapter 7: Presenting the benefits of an electronic portfolio and directing the reader through a step-by-step process to create an electronic portfolio

Chapter 8: Discussing ways to keep the portfolio alive beyond credential programs

2

Using Portfolios as Tools for Authentic Assessment and Evaluation

"Fairness" does not exist when assessment is uniform, standardized, impersonal, and absolute. Rather, it exists when assessment is appropriate—in other words, when it's personalized, natural, and flexible; when it can be modified to pinpoint specific abilities and function at the relevance of difficulty; and when it promotes a rapport between examiner and student.

—Funderstanding Web site, http://www.funderstanding.com/

Chapter Objectives

Readers will be able to

- define authentic assessment and evaluation,
- outline elements of the portfolio process as formative evaluations,
- identify elements of the portfolio process as summative evaluations,
- discuss the benefits of portfolios as both action research and authentic assessment,
- apply appropriate precautions in using portfolios for assessment and evaluation,

- use portfolios for both formative and summative evaluation,
- follow guidelines for using rubrics linked to standards for portfolio assessment.

Scenario

As part of their course culmination, teacher credential candidates presented final portfolios to their professor and peers in a formal presentation. Included in the presentations were answers to questions regarding the organization of their portfolios, the specific rationale for their selected artifacts, the value of courses and assignments in preparing these future teachers, and the portfolio process as a tool in assessing their individual growth and development throughout the program. Lisa, one of the teaching interns, reflected on her experience of the portfolio process:

"Through the assignments and other activities, I saw leadership qualities in myself that I may not have taken note of before, such as developing unit plans to teach science and math or having a classroom management plan that included my teaching philosophy and views on discipline. I probably would never have saved letters of commendation from supervisors and peers or taken pictures of bulletin boards I created if I had not been forced to keep a portfolio. As I collected artifacts for each teaching standard, I got a better understanding of what the standard was and how that standard was vital to my professional development as a teacher. Keeping a portfolio was almost like doing research on how I was becoming a teacher! Things that I thought were good lesson plans at the beginning of the program were thrown out by the end as I learned how to plan better lessons. I got to evaluate my own work in deciding what made the best evidence of proving I could teach, and what artifacts to keep in my final portfolio.

"Keeping a portfolio also helped me to monitor my growth on a daily basis as a formative assessment for each standard. Not only did it help me to define the standard, but it also helped me use specific criteria for assessing or evaluating that standard. Reflecting and presenting the final portfolio helped me to see the summative or overall growth of each standard working together in my overall development as a teacher."

Across the way, a similar conversation was taking place among a group of administrative credential candidates who were also in a final portfolio presentation session. Rogelio was among the first to comment on the portfolio process:

"When I first heard of the portfolio, I thought—'No problem!' I'm a teacher and I've used portfolios in my school with my elementary students. I know how helpful they are for showing growth in my elementary students and helping them to evaluate themselves. Still, I did not really understand

what I was in for as an administrative credential candidate. Portfolios are a Lot of Work!!! The process really helped me to think about what I was doing in each class and why, and how that class or assignment would help me to grow as an administrator. The portfolio helped me to stay focused on the big picture of becoming a school principal. Having to keep and organize assignments into artifacts also helped me to think more deeply about each assignment and how it assisted me in developing skills and abilities as an administrator. I was constantly putting myself through a microscope to view and evaluate my progress. Completing an assignment was not enough until I figured out what that assignment or activity had to do with my overall profile as an administrator or educational leader. When I developed a workshop for paraprofessionals on legal issues surrounding their roles and responsibilities, I saw how this one activity addressed several administrative standards. The portfolio process helped me to clearly identify each standard and to cross-reference assignments, artifacts, and activities when appropriate. The workshop I presented addressed community outreach, instructional leadership, as well as technology."

Overview

What is meant by the terms *formative* and *summative* when applied to assessment, and what role does the portfolio play in each of these kinds of assessment? From the scenario, it is evident that students benefit from the portfolio process as a formative, developmental assessment as they are advancing through their credential program. Similarly, students also benefit from collaboratively reflecting on the portfolio process as a summative, final assessment or overall evaluation of their performance at the completion of the program. The purpose of this chapter is to examine the role of portfolios in both formative and summative assessment and evaluation and to highlight the value of the portfolio for each type of assessment. This chapter is also designed to explore the portfolio process as a type of *action research,* in which educators seek ways to observe and improve their own practice (Mills, 2003; Newman, 2000). In this way, as portfolios are developed, they will be viewed as a magnifying lens into one's own growth and professional development. The portfolio is a powerful tool for self-assessment, goal setting, and future planning in how to improve.

The chapter begins with a brief definition of authentic assessment and evaluation. There are definitions of action research and inquiry and the prominent role authentic assessment and evaluation play in each of these concepts. The chapter continues with a description of the portfolio process and its benefits as a formative assessment. Next, some critical issues are presented on the role of portfolios as summative, high-stakes assessments for licensure and certification purposes, such as completing a teaching or other type of credential. Precautions and recommendations are presented to promote the most effective use of portfolios for authentic assessment and evaluation. The chapter concludes with guidelines for developing and following rubrics as a means of establishing consistent and specific criteria for clarifying portfolio expectations and evaluating portfolios.

Defining Assessment and Evaluation

Before going any further, it is important to clarify what is meant by the terms *evaluation* and *assessment* and how they are used in this book. Most dictionaries use these words interchangeably as synonyms (Landau & Bogus, 1975; Morris, 1976). Often, they are used to refer to the same processes; that is, to evaluate is also to examine or judge. This involves determining the value of a person or thing in relation to others of the same kind. Similarly, to assess is also to estimate the value of something or someone. It means to appraise or to form a judgment of worth or significance. In both cases, specific criteria need to be established as a basis for forming judgments of overall worth or value. In this book, the term *assessment* is used to refer to the ongoing, developmental process of growth and change. It refers to the formative, progressive nature of determining one's growth in a particular skill or area. Table 2.1 contrasts formative assessment and summative evaluations.

Table 2.1 Contrasting Formative Assessment and Summative Evaluation

Formative Assessment	*Summative Evaluation*
Pretest	Posttest
Posttest on assignment or activity	
Quizzes, grades on course assignments	Final exam
Attendance and participation in course	
Midterm	
Peer evaluations	Final grade in a course
Lesson plans, research reports	
Program coursework, fieldwork, and exams	Comprehensive exam
	High-stakes test
Working portfolio	Showcase portfolio
Entrance interview	Exit interview

For example, students often do a pretest or preassessment in a class to determine their background knowledge on a particular subject or skill. Preassessments are often used to establish baseline data, or a starting point, from which to measure growth. Later, after instruction has taken place, the same test can be used as a posttest to determine what has been learned. By comparing the results on the pre- and posttests, the instructor can see how much the student learned as a result of instruction or course activities. A midterm exam is another type of formative assessment to determine how a student is doing in a course at the halfway mark. It is a way to give a progress report on the knowledge and skills acquired by the student midway through the course. Similarly, when someone goes to the doctor, his or her temperature and blood pressure are taken as assessments of health. These data help the doctor to determine some basic information about a patient's health before going on to determine other areas of concern. If the temperature or blood pressure is higher or lower than normal, a more severe, possibly life-threatening health situation might be indicated.

Evaluation, on the other hand, is used to describe the final or summative process of determining one's overall progress in attaining minimal standards in a skill or field of study. A final grade, unlike the midterm, represents a summative or overall evaluation of a student's performance in the course. It results from collecting information from all other data sources used to assess a student's progress and performance, such as attendance, class participation, special projects, research reports, and a midterm exam. The final portfolio presentation session, described in the opening scenario for this chapter and discussed in more detail in Chapters 6 and 8, is an example of a summative assessment or overall evaluation. Students were sharing their completed portfolios and the impact of the portfolio process on their overall professional development in their credential programs. Evaluation usually takes place at the end and is the culmination of a series of skills and activities emphasized throughout a program or course of study. Showcase and academic portfolios may serve as summative evaluations of candidates and may be reviewed as partial fulfillment of the overall credential requirements. Evaluation is done as the final step in determining one's overall qualification to fulfill the responsibilities of a teacher, a counselor, or a principal.

Portfolios, which are organized collections of authentic artifacts or work samples, in which the candidate systematically demonstrates his or her completion of specific assignments, competencies, and standards over time, can be used effectively for both formative and summative aspects of assessment and evaluation. The working portfolio, described in Chapter 1, serves as a formative, developmental assessment, in which candidates select certain assignments or artifacts to include from various courses in their credential program. This working portfolio shows a candidate's progress up to that point in the program. As the candidate continues developing knowledge, skills, and dispositions as a teacher, counselor, or principal, new artifacts are included that provide better demonstrations of more recent competencies while others are eliminated. This process of systematically selecting and refining what to include in the portfolio is discussed in more detail in Chapter 4. The showcase portfolio, also described in Chapter 1, serves as a summative evaluation for the candidate, in which the best evidence of that candidate's qualifications is presented. In the opening scenario for this chapter, candidates were discussing their academic showcase portfolios, which they developed from their working portfolios in various credential programs.

Portfolios as Authentic Assessment: A Definition

Assessments are *authentic* when they have meaning in and of themselves, when the learning they measure has value beyond the classroom, and when learning is also meaningful to the learner (Kerka, 1995; Wiggins, 1999). Determining real-life examples and applications of competencies is the primary aim of *authentic assessment.* An example would be a high school student's ability to formally debate an issue, such as student-centered versus teacher-centered classrooms, as authentic evidence of his or her understanding and implementation of persuasive writing. Authentic assessment addresses the skills and abilities needed to perform actual tasks (e.g., writing and implementing a lesson plan, for teachers; conducting a program evaluation, for administrators; and coordinating a mediation meeting between a student and his parents, for school counselors). As reported in Chapter 1, portfolios afford students opportunities to display genuine examples of their achievement and to reflect on the value of those examples through written documentation.

For teachers, the process of setting up a supportive classroom environment, where there is a social contract between students and teachers regarding appropriate behavior, can be assessed in a variety of ways. This would fall under Principle 5: Classroom Motivation and Management, in the Interstate New Teacher Assessment and Support Consortium (INTASC) standards. The organization INTASC is a consortium of more than thirty states operating under the Council of Chief State School Officers (CCSSO) that has developed standards and an assessment process for initial teacher certification (Campbell, Melenyzer, Nettles, & Wyman, 2000). For example, a teacher could take a traditional exam, which asks the teacher to list or describe characteristics of effective classroom management, or, as a more authentic example of INTASC Principle 5, the teacher could show a video clip of classroom interaction with students and include a sketch of the classroom floor plan in the classroom management plan. A *classroom management plan* is an assignment in some teacher credential courses in which candidates describe their rationale for proposing a management system that would be appropriate for them. Some sample classroom management plans, along with instructions for how to create them, are found on the CD. These provide a more comprehensive example of the candidate's knowledge, skills, and dispositions in the area of classroom management than the answer to a simple test question ever could. Table 2.2 compares traditional assessment with authentic assessment.

Table 2.2 Traditional Versus Authentic Assessment

Traditional Assessment	*Authentic Assessment*
Quizzes and exams	Lesson plans
Checklists	Lesson study
Supervisor evaluations	Observation reports, field notes/ reflections
Exit interviews	Letters, cards from parents, students
Transcripts	Video clips
Comprehensive exams	Assignment reflections
Grades, grade point average (GPA)	Self-evaluations
	Peer evaluations
	Supervisor evaluations and reflections
	Classroom management plans
	Case studies
	Pictures of bulletin boards
	Organizational charts
	Examples of public school student work
	Letters of commendation
	Workshops developed by candidates
	Participant evaluations of workshops
	Philosophy of education
	Program evaluation plans
	Exit interviews
	Focus groups

Other examples might be actual letters of commendation and acknowledgment from principals or supervisors after having observed a teacher in the classroom and witnessed his or her effective management. These authentic examples, which become artifacts in the portfolio, provide a more comprehensive view from which to assess whether a teacher can practically apply the knowledge, skills, and dispositions measured by the standard. Rogelio, the administrative credential candidate in our opening scenario, commented on how his paraprofessional workshop on legal issues (another example of authentic assessment) addressed several administrative standards, such as ISLLC (Interstate School Leaders Licensure Consortium) Leadership Standard 5 (Human Resource Administration) and Leadership Standard 3 (Organizational Management). More examples of authentic assessment in the portfolio process are presented in Chapters 3, 4, 5, and 6.

Defining Action Research and Inquiry: Tools for the Educator Researcher

A common question among educators is, What exactly is action research, and what role does it play in portfolio development and authentic assessment? To begin, *action research,* in the most general sense of the term, is defined as a systematic approach used to improve one's own practice (McNiff, 2003; Reason & Bradbury, 2004; Sagor, 2003). It is further defined as the systematic execution of carefully articulated processes of inquiry or questioning, which is its strength (Mills, 2003; Stringer, 2004).

Therefore, action research is viewed as any systematic inquiry conducted by teachers, principals, and school counselors to gather information with the purpose of gaining insight, developing reflective practice, and effecting positive changes. Holly, Arhar, and Kasten (2005) described the action research journey as a process to make daily practice more professional by enabling us to focus on and prioritize what we most value and seek to achieve. Psychologist Kurt Lewin is often cited as originating action research when he used this methodology in 1944 in his work with people affected by postwar social problems. His goal in conducting action research was to promote social action through democratic decision making and active participation of practitioners in the research process. People were encouraged to see themselves as the resources for improving their own situations by systematically questioning, observing, and setting up strategies and interventions to change their behaviors and outcomes in positive ways. Action research has often been defined as the marriage between research and investigation, or between conducting inquiry, on the one hand, and action or practice, on the other.

Riding, Fowell, and Levy (1995) pointed out that action research has evolved into many forms, each involving an interactive approach, including problem identification; action planning to improve the problem; implementation of the action plan; or intervention, evaluation, and reflection. Action research methodology in education offers a systematic approach to introducing innovations in teaching and learning. Its goal is to place the educator in the dual role of (1) researcher or producer of educational theory and (2) practitioner or user of that theory to improve teaching and learning (McNiff & Whitehead, 2005).

The continuous sorting and selecting of artifacts to include or withdraw from the portfolio (i.e., to demonstrate the candidate's knowledge, skills, and dispositions) is, in essence, a personal type of action research involving continuous self-assessment and evaluation. In portfolio development, as in action research and inquiry, the candidate is continually seeking authentic, real-life examples of his or her own practice. He or she is continually asking whether or not particular artifacts best demonstrate the candidate's growth and transformation throughout the credential program. The candidate is constantly seeking to perfect his or her skills and to document those skills and knowledge through the portfolio process.

Like action research, the portfolio process is cyclical in nature, as Figure 2.1 demonstrates. Where possible, action research projects go through several cycles or spirals, each involving some form of inquiry or questioning. The primary question—How do I improve my work?—includes a social intent (McNiff, 2003; Mills, 2003). That is, improving one's work is meant not only for personal benefit but also for the benefit of others. If individuals can improve what they are doing, they can likely influence situations related to this work, whether it be in teaching, serving as an administrator, or school counseling. In addition, action research is viewed as a type of ongoing inquiry or investigation into strategies that can improve one's practice on multiple levels, similar to those described in the next section.

Levels of Action Research in Portfolio Development

According to McNiff (2003), there are six action research levels. These six levels parallel the same action research cycles identified by a number of researchers, although different terms may be used (Holly et al., 2005; Mills, 2003; Stringer, 2004). At the first level, *Problem Identification,* the question involves deciding what to place into the portfolio and why. That is, what artifacts provide accurate assessments and evidence for each standard?

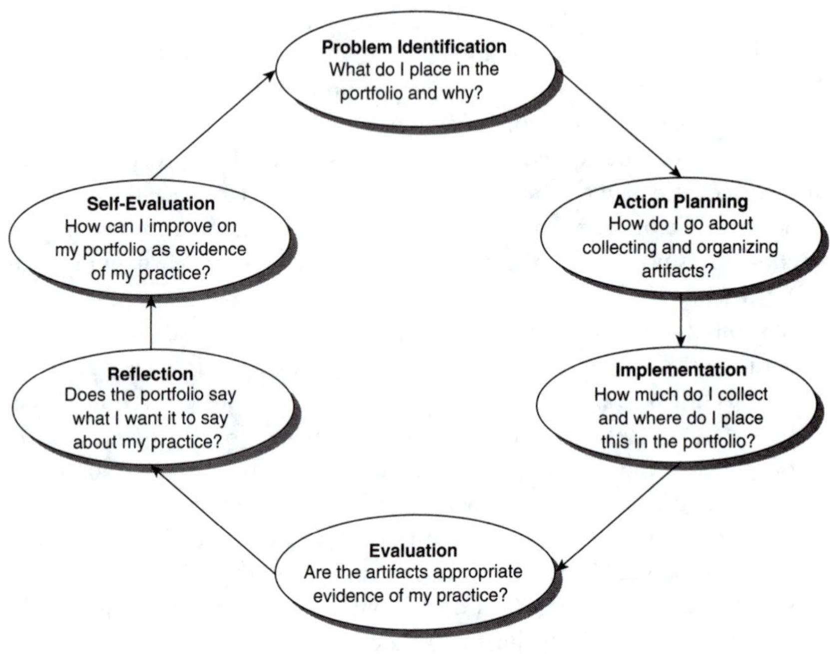

Figure 2.1 Cycle of Action Research Applied to Portfolio Development

At the second level, *Action Planning,* the inquiry is focused on deciding how to go about collecting and organizing authentic evidence for each standard. It involves laying out a plan for collecting and organizing artifacts. It further involves clarifying the standards and determining authentic experiences in the credential program through which the knowledge, skills, and dispositions are developed. This helps make each course more relevant in the overall credential preparation and each assignment more authentic in shaping the overall professional development of the candidate. This process of organizing the portfolio is discussed in more detail in Chapter 4.

At the third level, *Implementation,* the candidate actually goes about collecting the evidence according to the plan, all the while asking how much to collect and where to place it in the portfolio for the best display of evidence for each standard.

Moving on to the fourth level, *Evaluation,* the candidate reflects on the items placed in the portfolio and decides whether or not they provide appropriate evidence for the standards, or if other artifacts would be more effective for demonstrating the desired competencies and characteristics of the standards. The candidate also reflects on the process used to collect and organize the artifacts. Is the plan working? How can it be modified, if necessary?

At the fifth level, *Reflection,* the candidate reflects on the original purpose of the portfolio and decides if it lives up to its purpose: Does the portfolio say what I want it to say about my practice as a teacher, administrator, or counselor? If not, why not?

At the sixth level, *Self-Evaluation,* the candidate asks how the portfolio can be improved to provide the best evidence of the candidate's knowledge, skills, and dispositions. In answering these questions, the systematic process begins again, in the form of a spiral, with each cycle introducing a higher level of questioning and of perfecting the portfolio (McNiff, 2003; Mills, 2003, Stringer, 2004). As will be discussed in Chapters 3, 4, 5, and 6, the action research aspects of the portfolio can also be done collaboratively as the candidate receives feedback from peers, instructors, and mentors. Collaborative feedback on the portfolio is valuable at both the formative and summative assessment levels.

When action research is applied to the portfolio process, authentic examples of the candidate's practice become the data or *products* of his or her research. These products are authentic examples of the candidate's knowledge, skills, and dispositions. They are then compiled into a portfolio as artifacts. As the candidate researches his or her own practice to identify the most appropriate evidence of his or her abilities, understanding, attitudes, and beliefs, the portfolio becomes the template for painting a comprehensive portrait of the candidate as a professional.

As an example, a teacher credential candidate may place samples of lesson plans into the portfolio. These artifacts demonstrate the candidate's ability to plan effective lessons. This is according to INTASC Principle 7: Instructional Planning Skills. A full list of INTASC Standards appears on the CD. The teacher plans instruction based on knowledge of subject matter, students, the community, and curriculum goals (Campbell et al., 2000). Table 2.3 applies the action research steps in posing inquiry questions related to INTASC Principle 7, Instructional Planning Skills.

At the beginning of the credential program, the lesson plans placed in the portfolio may be rather basic, demonstrating only a fundamental understanding of how to teach academic areas such as math or social studies. As the candidate continues to grow, however, the quality of his or her lesson planning improves; the plans begin to show greater detail of classroom organization and student interaction with the subject matter. The candidate can then reflect on the artifacts placed into the portfolio. He or she strives to assess and evaluate the value of lesson plans produced later in the program

Table 2.3 Action Research Cycle Applied to INTASC Principle 7 (Instructional Planning)

Action Research Step	*Related Inquiry Questions on Instructional Planning*
Problem Identification	What is appropriate evidence of instructional planning (e.g., lesson plans, unit plans, case studies)?
Action Planning	Where in the program can evidence of instructional planning be collected (e.g., courses, fieldwork, assignments)?
Implementation	How many examples of instructional planning should be collected, and will they demonstrate more than one standard? Where do I place them in the portfolio, and what supporting documentation should I include to explain their purpose?
Evaluation	Are the examples of instructional planning that I've included the best evidence of my personal skills in instructional planning? Do they provide a range of my skills in instructional planning?
Reflection	Do the examples of instructional planning that I've included say what I want them to say about my professional knowledge, skills, and attitudes?
Self-Evaluation	How can I improve on my professional profile in the area of instructional planning? What additional skills do I need to grow? What other artifacts would provide stronger evidence?

SOURCE: Adapted from Action Research steps by McNiff (2003). Reprinted with permission.

in comparison with earlier plans, in terms of which provide better evidence of the standard and the candidate's development.

The later plans may be more complex and demonstrate new interventions the candidate implemented, once he or she had a better grasp of the subject matter, the students, and the variety of ways the subject could be taught to students. Examples of plan upgrades might include providing home links so that parents can participate in the lesson. For instance, parents may be encouraged to help their children recognize and remind them of environmental print around the home and community (e.g., food labels/packaging, fast food restaurant logos, road signs, advertising logos, and toy trademarks—the print we recognize from the colors, pictures, and shapes that surround it) as reinforcement for a literacy lesson at school. Similarly, later lesson plans may include applications of technology, such as students taking virtual tours of museums around the world as part of a world history lesson.

Later plans could also provide evidence of a variety of INTASC principles, such as Principle 3 (Adapting Instruction to Individual Needs) and Principle 4 (Using Multiple Instructional Strategies). Similarly, a candidate may include his or her philosophy of education at the beginning of the credential program as evidence of Principle 9 (Professional Commitment and Responsibility). Yet, by the end of the program, the original philosophy of education may have been pulled completely and replaced with a more current one that is supported with the candidate's real-life experiences in the field of education.

Benefits of Portfolios as Authentic Assessments

There are still more benefits of portfolios as authentic assessment. First, as noted in Chapter 1, they provide greater equity in evaluation of culturally and linguistically diverse candidates than do more traditional forms of testing. Portfolios can provide evidence of equity by aligning authentic real-world examples of knowledge, skills, and dispositions to specific standards. Well-designed portfolios provide a rich array of what candidates know and are able to do. They display both the products of learning (e.g., lesson plans and case studies) and the processes or reflections associated with each artifact. Portfolios are also able to accommodate different learning styles as well as acknowledge multiple ways of demonstrating competence, unlike tests or other traditional assessments.

Second, portfolios provide an internal, candidate-centered focus on artifacts and specific criteria. These criteria are thus aligned with the standards in which candidates are actively involved, such as the collection and documentation of their own achievement data linking theory to practice. This action research approach helps candidates to become more aware of their process and encourages ownership of their program (McNiff, 2003; Mills, 2003). They see the benefits of a systematic process for helping them to evaluate and assess their own strategies. In addition, candidates are encouraged to collaborate with peers for deeper insight into how to improve their portfolios and the documentation of their professional performance. This collaboration affords multiple opportunities of self-evaluation and improvement.

Third, portfolios allow for ongoing collaboration and reflection among the author, the assessors, and the evaluators, entailing a more relational process. Portfolios provide a tool that can ensure communication and accountability to a range of audiences. This type of interactive, dynamic process among instructors and learners is again more appropriate, equitable, and culturally responsive for candidates from diverse cultural and linguistic backgrounds (Johnson, 2002; Robins, Lindsey, Lindsey, & Terrell, 2005). Further, the overall portfolio process encourages ongoing and sustained dialogue among program instructors and students as they continue to refine the process and clarify the criteria used to measure success and effective completion of program standards and requirements. Evaluation standards must be clear, concise, and openly communicated.

Fourth, portfolios allow for multiple levels of assessment and evaluation, including self-assessment, peer assessment, mentor assessment, and supervisor/evaluator assessment, over extended periods of time. Because portfolio assessment is longitudinal and emphasizes the process of change or growth at multiple points in time, it may be easier to see patterns (Sewell et al., 2005). The types of feedback resulting from such a process allow for all participants to consider the next steps for improving both teaching and learning (Kerka, 1995). To be most effective, portfolios as authentic assessment need to be an integral part of the program and linked to all courses in the program. The portfolio process is thus a dynamic process that constantly goes through dialogue, revision, and modification. Organizing and implementing the portfolio process is discussed further in Chapter 4.

Challenges of Portfolios as Authentic Assessments

Although numerous advantages accompany the use of portfolios as authentic assessment, there are several drawbacks or challenges that must be mentioned. Among the challenges, the following are the three most prevalent:

- Managing the time-intensive nature of portfolio development
- Ensuring curriculum validity and reliability
- Minimizing evaluator bias and inconsistency

There is no doubt that portfolios are time-consuming both to prepare and to evaluate because they require clarity in goals, outcomes, criteria, and expectations and assurance that all stakeholders understand (Pennsylvania Assessment Through Themes, 2000; Wilkerson & Lang, 2003). To adequately prepare credential candidates and their instructors with the necessary time to manage the portfolio, the portfolio process must be emphasized throughout the program. This means spelling out careful guidelines and benchmarks that are understood and agreed upon by all stakeholders, along with building in support for meeting the standards and criteria. To ensure curriculum validity and reliability, both assessment and instruction should be planned concurrently to make certain that they are linked (Kerka, 1995; Wiggins, 1999). Grant Wiggins, in his Understanding by Design program (Wiggins & McTighe, 2000), referred to this process as "backwards planning." In backwards planning, one begins with the standard or the outcome, then works backward to determine indicators or assessments for those outcomes, and, lastly, plans instruction that will lead to those indicators and outcomes.

In addition, to ensure that evaluation standards are applied consistently, instructors and other raters or evaluators of the portfolio need careful training and collaboration on the process. Staff development and ongoing dialogue regarding evaluation criteria must be part of the full portfolio implementation process. At the course level, instructors present clear definitions of program and course expectations to candidates in their syllabi. They also indicate how these expectations relate to assignments in the course and to meeting program standards. This is a good time also to describe which assignments may be used as possible portfolio artifacts, along with how each assignment will be evaluated. Rubrics should be provided to add further clarity of expectations and grading criteria. More will be discussed on rubrics later in this chapter.

Portfolios as Formative (Developmental Process) Assessments

There are numerous aspects of portfolios that make them extremely desirable and effective as developmental assessments over time (Campbell, Cignetti, Melenyzer, Nettles, & Wyman, 2004). Such portfolios are often viewed as *process* or *working portfolios*, described in Chapter 1, which document growth over time toward a goal. Documentation includes statements of the end goals, criteria, and plans for the future. The process or working portfolio, as a formative assessment, is most useful for the internal information of the candidates and instructors as they plan for the future. It is an excellent tool for reinforcing learning and for making formative decisions about candidate knowledge, skills, dispositions, and growth, as well as the programs that prepare them (Wilkerson & Lang, 2003; Sewell et al., 2005). Individual course assignments are usually targeted for inclusion in the working portfolio as demonstrations of course goals and objectives and of overall credential program outcomes. In a teacher credential course, for example, candidates must demonstrate their ability to tailor their teaching style to the individual needs and learning styles of their students, as in INTASC Principle 3 (Adapting Instruction for Individual Needs) and Principle 4 (Multiple Instructional Strategies). They must also demonstrate a value and sensitivity to diversity, as in INTASC Principle 2 (Knowledge of Human Development and Learning). For instance, completing a *case study* as an assignment (e.g., the candidate not only diagnoses oral language and reading ability of an elementary or middle school student, but also plans appropriate reading and oral language interventions to support that student's growth) addresses all three INTASC principles. Such an assignment is a natural fit for inclusion in the working portfolio. McNiff (2003) describes a five-tiered action research approach, which can be applied to the portfolio development process. This five-tiered approach best illustrates how the actual portfolio process has inherent advantages in the formation and development of any program, as outlined in Table 2.4.

Table 2.4 Five-Tiered Approach to Program Development and Portfolio Assessment

Tier 1—Program Definition	Clarifying program goals, standards, and desired outcomes
Tier 2—Accountability	Agreeing on appropriate forms of evidence and how they will consistently be collected and evaluated in portfolio process
Tier 3—Understanding and Refining	Conducting ongoing assessment of the program and candidates at regular portfolio checkpoints to refine, modify, and align outcomes with the program vision
Tier 4—Progress Toward Outcomes	Collecting and reviewing evidence in portfolios at regular intervals throughout the program in the form of dialogues among program participants to ensure consistency and reliability
Tier 5—Program Impact	Cumulatively collecting a broad band of evidence through the portfolio process to form a summative evaluation of overall program impact

SOURCE: Adapted from McNiff (2003). Reprinted with permission.

At Tier 1, *Program Definition,* thinking about portfolio criteria may assist in clarifying program goals, objectives, and desired outcomes. It can also assist in forging a vision and purpose for the program.

At Tier 2, *Accountability,* the portfolio is considered an assessment practice that informs all constituents about appropriate forms of *evidence,* which serve as criteria for accountability. The process of identifying and selecting evidence involves ongoing dialogue and feedback among all stakeholders involved in developing the portfolio. When candidates and instructors agree on expectations and goals, there is greater acceptance and satisfaction with program activities because the purpose is clear.

At Tier 3, *Understanding and Refining,* the portfolio provides a means of conducting ongoing assessments of the program and/or the participants, as the program addresses evolving needs and assets of those involved. This process of refining helps to maintain a focus on program outcomes, the steps needed to attain these outcomes, and assurance that the program implementation is in line with the vision.

At Tier 4, *Progress Toward Outcomes,* it is most effective to select and provide evidence of progress toward specific outcomes at regular intervals throughout the program, in the context of conferences and dialogues among program participants. These intervals can be scheduled at the end of courses, midway through the program, and at the conclusion of the program. These types of regular portfolio checkpoints and timelines are discussed more fully in Chapter 4. This reinforces the collaborative nature of the portfolio process and supports consistency and reliability of the evidence.

At Tier 5, *Program Impact,* all of the earlier levels work together to communicate overall program impact to those outside the program. Through the portfolio, a broad range of evidence has been collected over time to determine (a) if the program has met its goals and (b) what the overall effect of the program and goals has been for the participants involved. This type of evidence, including successes of individuals or programs, can be very persuasive and influential to policymakers, funders, community members, and agencies for accreditation and licensing (Sewell et al., 2005; Wilkerson & Lang, 2003).

Portfolios as Summative (Final Product) Evaluations

Some of the main concerns regarding portfolios occur when they are used in summative, high-stakes evaluations (Bateson, 1994; Sewell et al., 2005; Wilkerson & Lang, 2003). *High-stakes evaluations* are those in which tests or other devices such as portfolios are used to make high-stakes decisions.

For example, candidates may be granted or denied a diploma, certificate, or license based on the results of the evaluation. Summative "product" portfolios (also known as *showcase* or *employment* portfolios) include *final evidence,* or items that demonstrate attainment of the end goals.

Wilkerson and Lang (2003) cautioned that portfolios could be used as an appropriate and safe vehicle to make summative decisions in a certification context only as long as the contents are rigorously controlled and systematically evaluated. When decisions are standards-based, summative, and meant to result in initial certification, minimal competency must be established. In licensure, the state must ensure that candidates are "safe" to enter the profession and will effectively carry out its responsibilities. Summative product portfolios must contain evidence that demonstrates the candidate's ability to fulfill his or her responsibilities in the profession. Portfolio assessments, when used as summative evaluations to make licensure decisions, must stand the tests of validity, reliability, fairness, and absence of bias.

Precautions and Recommendations for Effective Practice in Portfolio Evaluation

In light of the earlier discussion of the role of portfolios in both formative and summative evaluation, it is important to outline a few precautions and recommendations for effective practice in portfolio evaluation. Wilkerson and Lang (2003) recommend eight requirements for the construction of portfolios as summative evaluations used for certification in a school, a college, or a department of education (SCDE). These are summarized in Table 2.5.

As with any other qualitative assessment, care must be taken in collecting, evaluating, and reporting the results. Methods of analysis will vary depending on the purpose of the portfolio and the types of data collected. This information needs to be clarified and specified at the beginning of the portfolio process. When goals and criteria are clearly defined, it is relatively easy to demonstrate that the candidate has moved from a baseline level of performance to achievement of particular goals. To reduce subjectivity of judgments, portfolio assessment and portfolios should be periodically and independently rated. This provides a check on reliability, which can be simply reported. For example, a local programmer could say, "To ensure some consistency in assessment standards, every 5th (or 20%) was assessed by more than one instructor. Agreement between raters, or interrater reliability, was 88%" (Sewell et al., 2005).

Table 2.5 Requirements for Portfolio Use in Certification Testing

1. Knowledge, skills and dispositions must be essential and authentic representations of job-related behaviors.
2. Portfolio must be representative of, relevant to, and proportional to the profession, and criteria used to evaluate the portfolio must be relevant to the job.
3. Candidates must be provided in advance with adequate written guidelines and procedures for compiling the portfolio. These guidelines must include how and when to prepare the portfolio, how it will be reviewed, who is allowed to help them, and how much help they can receive. They must also be notified of the consequences of failure, the opportunities for remediation, and their due-process rights and procedures should they wish to challenge the review results. In addition, candidates must be notified on the appeals process and assured of its fairness in design and implementation.
4. Instructional time must be built into the program for candidates to succeed in meeting the portfolio requirements and to remediate when performance is inadequate. The portfolio process should be embedded into the entire instructional program, and all instructors need to buy into and support the portfolio preparation activities.
5. Scoring rubrics used to guide the portfolio process must be realistic in determining acceptable performance. A specific score, or set of characteristics, needs to differentiate between those candidates who are competent, or demonstrate proficiency in the knowledge skills and dispositions to enter the profession, and those who are not.
6. Options and alternatives must be provided to candidates who cannot successfully complete specific portfolio requirements, or, in the case where there is no alternative, the SCDE must be able to demonstrate why no alternatives exist. Options and alternatives must be equitable and relate to specific artifacts in the portfolio. The institution must ensure that alternatives are also representative of, relevant to, and proportional to the profession.
7. Portfolio evaluation (scoring) in terms of equity of outcomes for protected populations (i.e., with differences based on culture, language, ability, gender, etc.) should be monitored.
8. The portfolio process must be designed, implemented, and monitored to ensure reliable scoring and to provide for necessary candidate support. Regular portfolio assessment checkpoints should be established for collaboration, with tests of reliability performed and samples of candidates' work and instructors' scoring reviewed regularly to ensure that they remain valid and consistent, and that measurement error is minimized. Portfolio scorers need to receive professional development in scoring and be updated on a regular basis. Directions should be clear and consistent.

SOURCE: Concepts adapted from Wilkerson & Lang (2003).

Rubrics for Portfolio Assessment

The *rubric* is a tool used in authentic assessment to assess or establish criteria that are complex and subjective (Goodrich, 1997; Lazear, 1998; Popham, 1997; Wiggins, 1999). The rubric is designed to simulate real-life activity, such that students are engaged in solving problems such as classroom management or lesson planning. Effective rubrics also help to define and quantify successful levels of performance. According to Wiggins (1999), rubrics show levels of performance on a standard or skill over a continuum, ranging from high or expert level of performance to low or ineffective level of  performance. Sample rubrics are available later in this chapter, on the CD. The rubric is a formative type of assessment because it becomes an ongoing part of the entire teaching and learning process, as criteria are defined and quantified from high to low. Students can be actively engaged in the rubric design process, and as they become more familiar with the rubric, they can assist in its design. This involvement empowers students to become more focused and self-directed in their own learning. As a result, they have a much clearer idea of what is expected of them. Tables 2.6 and 2.7 describe the characteristics of rubrics as well as the advantages of using them in portfolio assessment based on prominent research findings (Goodrich, 1997; Popham, 1997; Wiggins, 1999).

Table 2.6 Characteristics of Rubrics

Rubrics are tools for

- communicating specific *expectations and grading criteria* based on examples;
- measuring or quantifying a *stated objective or standard* (e.g., performance, behavior, skill, or quality);
- assigning levels or using a *range* to score performance;
- describing the *degree or amount* to which a standard has been met based on ascending levels.

Table 2.8 provides an example of a rubric used to evaluate a thematic English language development (ELD) unit in a teacher credential program. Here, the instructor lays out specific criteria of the assignment and how the various criteria will be scored. The unit could later be placed in the portfolio

Table 2.7 Advantages of Effective Rubrics in Portfolio Assessment

Effective rubrics

- build more objectivity and consistency in assessment and evaluation;
- allow the instructor to clarify his or her grading criteria in specific terms with examples;
- demonstrate to students how their work will be evaluated and explain what is expected of them;
- provide students with clear targets in specific, measurable terms;
- assist students in being more self-directed and reflective;
- promote student awareness of the criteria to use in assessing peer performance;
- give useful feedback to instructors regarding the effectiveness of the instruction;
- outline benchmarks for measuring and documenting progress;
- offer students a greater sense of ownership for their learning;
- provide the opportunity to assess more student outcomes than traditional assessment does.

Table 2.8 Sample Thematic English Language Development (ELD) Unit Assessment Rubric

	Excellent	*Satisfactory*	*Needs Improvement*
Overview	3 pts. Conveys purpose clearly. Notes target grade. Introduces why topic is of interest to English-language learners. Notes length of unit.	2 pts. Conveys purpose. Notes target grade and length.	1 pt. Introduces unit but not grade level. Purpose or relevance is vague.
Unit Goals	2 pts. Goals clearly written. Goals cover a range of outcomes. State standards are cited, including ELD and related content standards.	1 pt. Goals are written.	0 pts. No goals are stated.

(Continued)

Table 2.8 (Continued)

	Excellent	*Satisfactory*	*Needs Improvement*
Assessment Instrument	4 pts. A reliable scale is developed (i.e., detailed, concrete, well-designed). Scale is appropriate for task. Task is explained clearly. Usage/data collection is explained clearly.	3 pts. A reliable scale is developed (i.e., detailed, concrete). Scale is appropriate for task. Usage/data collection is explained.	2 pts. A usable scale is developed. Scale is somewhat appropriate for task. Usage is explained.
Lesson Plans	12 pts. At least 5 plans are developed. Plans are clearly explained so that another could use them. Plans state 3 objectives written in correct format. Assessment is addressed. Plan format fits the proposed learning activities and is modified (i.e., differentiated) for each ELD level.	9 pts. At least 4 plans are developed. Plans are clearly explained so that another could use them. Plans state 3 objectives written in correct format and are modified (i.e., differentiated) for each ELD level.	6 pts. At least 3 plans are developed. Plans are clearly explained. Plans state 2 objectives and are modified (i.e., differentiated) for each ELD level.
Home Connection and Technology Applications	2 pts. There is a clear home connection in the unit, as well as applications of technology.	1 pt. There is a home connection in the unit.	0 pts. There is no home connection.
Resource/ Reference List	2 pts. There is a reference list at the end of the unit identifying all references and resources used to develop the unit, including related Web sites. Complete references are also stated on individual lesson plans where appropriate.	1 pt. Complete references are stated on individual lesson plans where appropriate.	0 pts. There is no reference list.

as an example of INTASC Principle 3 (Adapting Instruction for Individual Needs).

More sample rubrics are provided in Chapter 4 and on the CD.

Summary

From this discussion, it is clear that portfolios offer excellent tools for authentic assessment by providing real-life evidence of completion of program standards. They further expose candidates to a type of action research that is focused on helping the candidate improve his or her own practice in both formative, developmental assessment as well as summative evaluation. Still, despite their benefits, portfolios are not a panacea and require careful guidelines and collaboration to avoid pitfalls such as inconsistencies in definitions and expectations. The contents of portfolios must be rigorously controlled and systematically assessed. There must also be ongoing tests of validity, reliability, and fairness in scoring, particularly when portfolios are used as summative evaluations for licensure decisions. The use of rubrics helps the portfolio process to be more objective, consistent, and reliable. In the next chapter, we explore the role of reflection in giving voice to the portfolio beyond the mere collection of artifacts.

Useful Resources

The following resources will be useful in viewing grading criteria and designing sample rubrics for the portfolio:

Goodrich, H. (1997). Understanding rubrics. *Educational Leadership, 54*(4), 14–17.

Huffman, E. (1998). Authentic rubrics. *Art Education, 51*(1), 64–68.

Jensen, K. (1995). Effective rubric design: Making the most of this powerful tool. *Science Teacher, 62*(5), 72–75.

Lazear, D. (1998). *The rubrics way: Using MI to assess understanding*. Tucson, AZ: Zephyr Press.

Popham, W. (1997). What's wrong and what's right—with rubrics? *Educational Leadership, 55*(3), 72–75.

Rubrics for Web Lessons: http://edweb.sdsu.edu/webquest/rubrics/weblessons.htm

Taggart, G., Phifer, S., Nixon, J., & Wood, M. (Eds.). (1998). *Rubrics: A handbook for construction and use.* Lancaster, PA: Technomics.

Wiggins, G. (1999). *Educative assessment: Designing assessments to inform and improve student performance.* San Francisco: Jossey-Bass.

For Further Reading

Campbell, V. M., Cignetti, P. B., Melenyzer, B. J., Nettles, D. H., & Wyman, Jr., R. M. (2004). *How to develop a professional portfolio: A manual for teachers* (3rd ed.). Boston: Allyn & Bacon.

Hebert, E. A. (2001). *The power of portfolios: What children can teach us about learning and assessment.* San Francisco: Jossey-Bass.

Sagor, R. (2003). *Action research guidebook: A four-step process for educators and school teams.* Thousand Oaks, CA: Sage.

Wiggins, G. (1999). *Educative assessment. Designing assessments to inform and improve student performance.* San Francisco: Jossey-Bass.

Wiggins, G., & McTighe, J. (2000). *Understanding by design* (Rev. ed.). Alexandria, VA: Association of Supervision and Curriculum Development.

Wilkerson, J. R., & Lang, W. S. (2003, December 3). Portfolios, the pied piper of teacher certification assessments: Legal and psychometric issues. *Education Policy Analysis Archives, 11*(45).

3

The Portfolio as a Tool for Reflective Inquiry

Moving From Vision to Reality

We do not learn from experience. We learn from reflecting on experience.

—John Dewey

Chapter Objectives

Readers will be able to

- describe the four types of portfolio reflections;
- identify ten ways reflections transform "artifacts" into "evidence";
- recognize the multifaceted, cyclical nature of reflections;
- use guiding questions to lead reflective inquiry in the portfolio process;
- view reflections as a key component of action research;
- view reflections as the glue bonding the portfolio to a purpose;
- state the outcomes and benefits of reflective inquiry in portfolio development.

Scenario

Irma and Matt, two teaching credential candidates, have just entered their science methods course for the first time. As the syllabi are distributed and the professor begins to give an overview of the course, including the ongoing portfolio requirement, the following exchange occurs between the two:

Matt begins, "I've heard portfolios are just a waste of time; nobody looks at them anyway! I can't understand why we are required to do them. To me, it's just more busywork that gets in the way of real, practical activities. What can a portfolio teach me about working in school?"

Irma responds, "My portfolio has taught me a lot about myself and my values when it comes to teaching because I explain why I put in the different items. My portfolio really helped me to see how much I have changed since I began this program. It also helped me to focus! It was a lot of work at first, but now I'd be lost without it. The most important thing is that my portfolio helped me to get organized. When I first started, it seemed like I was just collecting a lot of 'stuff,' and I didn't see how it all related. Then, some of my professors explained different ways to set it up so that it told a story. They helped me to explain why I had put certain things into the portfolio and what I wanted the portfolio to say about me. Once I became clear regarding my purpose for having a portfolio, then the portfolio took on a life of its own. I also began to realize that you don't have to save everything in a portfolio and that there are different kinds of portfolios. You can set them up in different ways depending on your goals."

Later in the quarter, both Irma and Matt participated in a portfolio exchange conducted in the class, in which students exchanged portfolios with a peer. Once Matt saw the variety of ways portfolios could be organized, he began to realize how he could modify his own portfolio to present a clearer picture of who he was as a teacher. He noted the extra care with which Irma had developed her portfolio, such as her table of contents as outlined by the standards, careful reflection on each artifact, and use of pictures, parent letters, and more. Her portfolio definitely had a clear purpose and told a story, unlike his.

Overview

A major goal of this book is making the experience of developing and maintaining a portfolio one that is positive, relevant, and rewarding. Yet, the two contrasting viewpoints in the foregoing scenario are indicative of the possible range of responses toward being required to keep a portfolio in one's credential program. The candidates' statements are also indicative of the range of reactions that instructors receive when they announce the portfolio requirements for the courses they teach.

The question is, How does one transform the first, negative statements and experiences about portfolios into the second, affirming statements and experiences? What allows the portfolio process to become a valuable and meaningful experience for credential candidates and thus to perpetuate a lifelong practice of documentation and reflection? Another question is, How can credential candidates be supported in the process of developing professional portfolios in a way that will guide them throughout their education and subsequent careers? The answers to these questions lie in the use of carefully articulated reflections for clarifying the purpose of the portfolio and its contents.

In this chapter we aim to show the pivotal role that reflections play in the portfolio process, by linking isolated artifacts to specific purposes and thereby increasing the relevance of the portfolio (Barrett, 2001; Bartell, Kaye, & Morin, 1998; Burke, 1997; Wolf & Dietz, 1998).We illustrate how reflections breathe life into the portfolio by giving voice to the supporting action research, as discussed in Chapter 2. Also, we describe the process of reflective inquiry, or guiding reflections through questioning, to further clarify the rationale for each artifact and transform it into evidence of the candidates' professional beliefs and abilities (Burke, 1997; Dollase, 1996). As indicated by numerous researchers, both candidates and instructors must take ownership of the portfolios by relating them to their own personal and professional goals. This is required for candidates to see a personal benefit to portfolios (Grant & Huebner, 1998; McKinney, 1998; Schmuck, 1997; Wolf & Dietz, 1998). For credential candidates, this may be viewing the portfolio process as collecting evidence of their professional skills and knowledge in a particular program, lesson, or course (Burke, 1997; Dollase, 1996). For instructors, it may be viewing the portfolio as a tool for authentic assessment of a course or program (Barnett, 1992; Murray, 1997; Winsor & Ellefson, 1998), as discussed in Chapter 2. Both instances reinforce the concept of reflection as an essential component of the portfolio process.

This chapter begins with a brief definition of reflection and reflective inquiry as they relate to portfolio development. From there, it explores the top ten ways reflections transform "artifacts" into "evidence," as well as the multifaceted, cyclical nature of reflections. The chapter continues with a series of guiding questions to lead reflective inquiry. It then defines the levels of reflection that can be used to assess the overall quality of a portfolio in the form of a rubric. The chapter concludes with a review of the benefits and outcomes of reflections in portfolio development.

Four Types of Portfolio Reflections

We begin by asking, How does one define *reflections* in the portfolio process? Reflections are, in essence, captions or small statements and explanations that are used to give voice to the various artifacts that are collected in the portfolio (Barrett, 2000; Burke, 1997; Wolf & Dietz, 1998). There are four general types of portfolio reflections: goal statements, reflective statements, captions as statements, and assessment and evaluation statements. These reflections or statements are attached to each artifact, articulating what it is, why it is evidence, and what it is evidence of. These statements fall in the realm of reflective inquiry, which, in essence, is reflection guided by focused inquiry or questioning about the absolute value of each artifact to the portfolio (Grant & Huebner, 1998; McKinney, 1998). Samples of each type of statement are listed in Table 3.1.

Goal-setting statements refer to educational or professional goals that can be clearly articulated (i.e., career ladder/professional advancement/education). They further outline the purpose behind the portfolio.

Reflective statements can be the result of either personal reflection or collaborative reflection resulting from communications with mentors, supervisors, peers, professors, and so forth. Reflective statements provide general reactions or responses to the artifact, as well as a context for the artifact, clarifying its purpose in the portfolio. They further demonstrate the interactive nature of the portfolio, such as the individual interacting with the artifact, with the process, and with others during the portfolio process.

Captions as statements usually include explanations and identification that further provide a rationale for the inclusion of certain artifacts. They fall more in the category of labels, definitions, or explanation of artifacts. Captions can also state the source of the artifact, such as a course and its purpose in the overall credential program.

Authentic assessment and evaluation statements are formative and summative evaluative statements indicating growth or accomplishment in the targeted criteria or standards. These evaluative statements often make reference to the standards and discuss growth in comparison with the original goal of the portfolio. There may be some overlap in the purpose of the statements. Most important is the value of the statement in giving life and meaning to the artifacts.

Reflections take on many forms, from simple captions of two or three sentences that are used to identify an artifact, its source, and its purpose, to more elaborate explanations and definitions of the artifact's role in the portfolio. Table 3.2 provides examples of possible artifacts and their corresponding reflections.

Table 3.1 Samples of Four Types of Portfolio Reflections

Goal-Setting Statements: I am submitting this portfolio in partial fulfillment of my teaching credential. One of my professional goals in creating this portfolio is to secure a position as a school administrator. This portfolio demonstrates my competencies as a school psychologist, and it lays the foundation for my desire to enter the PhD program in counseling. One of my primary goals in completing this activity was . . .
Reflective Statements: I learned a great deal about myself through this assignment because . . . When I met with my supervisor after this field assignment, I discovered . . . This activity not only demonstrated my use of technology but also addressed . . . The feedback I received from my peers on this assignment was . . .
Captions as Statements: This is my resume, which shows my background in . . . This is a copy of my credential, which I included because . . . This is an award I received from . . . This is a letter of recommendation from . . .
Authentic Assessment and Evaluation Statements: The way(s) I have grown are demonstrated by . . . In the area of classroom management, I have grown in the following ways, as demonstrated by . . . I used this artifact as evidence of my skills in educational leadership in the area of leading individuals and groups toward common goals. I received the highest points possible in the multimedia presentation, which fulfilled both the technology and the community outreach standards.

SOURCE: Adapted from Pennsylvania Assessment Through Themes (PATT, 2000).

The author of a portfolio may explain what he or she learned as demonstrated by the artifact and how this information enhanced the overall portfolio process. For instance, the parent letter mentioned in Table 3.2 was used to support a middle school literacy program. It resulted in a 50 percent increase in parent participation. This is strong evidence of INTASC Principle 10 (Partnerships). Similarly, a math lesson plan can show various details of using multiple instructional strategies (INTASC Principle 4), such as manipulatives and higher-order questioning. These artifacts are much more powerful as a result of the reflections used to support them. The author of a

Table 3.2 Sample Artifacts and Corresponding Reflections

Artifact	*Reflections*
Philosophy of Education	This is my philosophy of education (EDUC 300), which continued to evolve throughout the program.
Parent Letter	This is a letter I wrote to the parents of my middle school students to encourage greater parental support in my literacy unit. As a result, I increased parental involvement by 50% (EDSE 415).
Paraprofessional Workshop on Testing	This is a workshop I conducted to help paraprofessionals understand the new testing procedures in our district. I developed a digital slideshow presentation to explain new procedures and laws regarding testing. I also attached evaluations of the workshop (EDAD 420).
Samples of Student Work	These are samples of student work from the sample lesson plan I wrote and taught. I used them to assess the students.
Lesson Plans (English Language)	This lesson plan demonstrates my ability to work with special populations in the area of English-language development.
Lesson Plans (Math)	This is my first attempt at a math lesson. Notice how the subsequent plans show much more variety in terms of use of manipulatives, higher-order thinking, and classroom organization.
Pictures of Bulletin Boards	These are pictures of bulletin boards I created to reinforce my lessons and enhance the classroom environment.
Science Learning Center	I developed this exploratory center on sound to help my elementary students have a hands-on experience in discovering how sound travels. The learning center helped me to individualize instruction and foster greater student responsibility.
Resume	This is a copy of my resume which I included to show my previous experience as a tutor and teaching assistant.
Workshop Flyers	These are copies of workshops I attended as evidence of INTASC Principle 9 (Professional Commitment and Responsibility).

portfolio may also simply identify an artifact, such as a resume or credential, without any further explanation other than the origin or date. It is best, however, to include the overall reflection and rationale for why those artifacts were selected for inclusion and how each adds texture to the candidate's professional profile.

Reflections require careful and serious thought and consideration. Such reflections are presented in written form in order to articulate or explain each artifact's purpose or value in the portfolio. Reflections, in a general sense, are thus a way of constructing meaning around past events for the purpose of informing actions in the present. Kay Burke (1997) further explained in her work *Designing Professional Portfolios for Change* that without reflections, or written commentaries, the portfolio is no more than a scrapbook and does not give insight into the criteria used to collect the artifacts. Kenneth Wolf and Mary Dietz (1998) go even further to emphasize the importance of reflections in their article "Teaching Portfolios: Purposes and Possibilities" when they state:

> More than anything else, the portfolio process should inspire reflection—alone and in the company of others. . . . Reflective commentaries by the portfolio owner are essential companion pieces to artifacts. Writing reflections pushes teachers to more deeply examine their practice and allows others to examine the thinking behind the teaching documented in the portfolio. . . . With reflection, the portfolio can become an episode of learning. (p. 14)

Reflections as an Essential Component of Action Research

As was mentioned in Chapter 2, reflections are an essential component of action research because they give voice to the underlying inquiry that guides the overall collection of artifacts. Their purpose is to answer the reflective inquiry questions that are posed at each level of the action research cycle (see Figure 2.1). Many artifacts, therefore, are eliminated before they ever reach the portfolio, as a result of reflective inquiry, which aims to identify only the most effective evidence to demonstrate the candidate's growth and development toward each standard.

Reflective inquiry is an aspect of action research in which the reflective process is guided by specific inquiry questions (McNiff, 2003). As Stephen Covey stated in his book *The 7 Habits of Highly Effective People* (1990), the first two steps toward effectiveness in any endeavor are "being proactive" and "beginning with the end in mind." This entails taking the initiative to set clear goals before beginning the work. In portfolio development, reflections work much the same way as taking these initial steps. Even before the first artifact is collected, one needs to reflect on the reasons for developing the portfolio and the nature of the desired outcomes. That is, What would make the portfolio be of value to you in your professional or personal life, or both? This, in large part, will determine what types of artifacts will be collected, what will be written about them, and how they will shape the overall portfolio (Campbell, Melenyzer, Nettles, & Wyman, 2000; Hurst, Wilson, & Cramer, 1998).

In addition, reflections and reflective inquiry can open up the process to new possibilities as candidates and instructors determine their individual desires for the portfolio and the types of artifacts and reflections to include. Reflections and reflective inquiry therefore involve *thinking about what* to put into the portfolio and *why,* as well as providing *the actual written statements* that accompany and explain the artifacts.

Reflections as Glue: Bonding the Portfolio to a Purpose

Hurst and colleagues (1998) referred to reflections as the "glue" bonding the portfolio to a specific purpose. Because there are numerous types of portfolios, including learning/working portfolios, assessment portfolios, and showcase/employment portfolios (see Chapter 1), the nature and role of reflections are vital for identifying the different types of portfolios (Hartnell-Young & Morriss, 1999; Wilcox & Tomei, 1999; Wolf, 1999). Further, reflections throughout the portfolio allow for extended possibilities of portfolios beyond assessment, learning, and professional development to their use as a "living history of a teaching-learning life." In the next section, we describe examples of how this use of portfolios is accomplished. One of the major advantages of reflections and reflective inquiry is that they promote ownership over the learning process by guiding the process through goal setting, focusing, and prioritizing possibilities (Danielson & Abrulyn, 1997; Gathercoal, Love, Bryde, & McKean, 2002; Stone, 1998; Wolf, 1999).

Ten Ways Reflections Transform Artifacts Into Evidence

It is well documented that the reflective process is not only both developmental and cyclical but also both formative and summative, as stated in

Chapter 2 (Barton & Collins, 1997; Campbell et al., 2000; Danielson & Abrulyn, 1997). Among the activities that one undertakes during the process of reflective inquiry, or questioning leading to a specific purpose or goal, is the cycle of projection, collection, selection, reflection, and back to projection for new direction and purposes. This process repeats, as is noted in subsequent chapters.

Building on this initial concept of reflective inquiry as a foundation, Table 3.3 describes ten related behaviors that further demonstrate the multifaceted nature of reflections. When one systematically builds a professional portfolio in a developmental and cyclical manner, based on these questioning practices and behaviors, artifacts are transformed slowly into evidence. In this process, each artifact is supported with a clear rationale stating its purpose in the context of the entire portfolio.

Artifacts are linked to specific purposes and goals within the portfolio through reflections. Reflections serve to clarify the portfolio documents and make the thinking process explicit. Reflective inquiry questions guide the process of collecting artifacts and documenting their purpose. Electronic portfolios provide the potential to create and provide links from multiple perspectives and multiple goals. This process is elaborated on in Chapter 7.

The Multifaceted, Cyclical Nature of Portfolio Reflection

To determine the value of reflection in the portfolio process, it is first important to examine the nature of reflection as a means of comprehending the types of roles that reflection can play. In this book, the term *reflective inquiry* is used along with the term *reflection* to differentiate the kinds of reflection that are based on structured inquiry and questioning strategies. Richard Schmuck (1997) discussed ten categories of reflective practice among maturing educators in conducting action research. These categories are listed in Table 3.4.

The categories of reflective practice coincide closely with the role reflections play in transforming "artifacts" into evidence by linking them with a purpose. A framework for reflective inquiry in the portfolio process results from merging the two views of reflection and adding guiding questions to better direct the portfolio reflection process at each phase. Questions also reinforce the continuous need for reflection at multiple levels. Reflective inquiry in portfolio development is actually action research guided by reflections and inquiry questions on how to identify and organize the artifacts in a portfolio. It is demonstrated in Table 3.5 and in Figure 3.1.

Table 3.3 Ten Ways Reflections Transform "Artifacts" Into "Evidence"

1. **Project** purposes of portfolio	Set clear goals and state them in reflections. *What purpose will the artifact serve? What will it say about me?*
2. **Collect** and organize artifacts with captions	Insert labels for rationale of artifacts—giving voice. *How do I identify each artifact? Its source? What does it say about my knowledge, skills, and dispositions?*
3. **Select** key artifacts	Prioritize and include rationale. *Why am I including these artifacts, and what purpose do they serve?*
4. **Interject** personality	Incorporate style and tone in reflections. *How can I personalize these artifacts to show my unique style?*
5. **Reflect** metacognitively	Insert formative statements. *How does this artifact reflect my growth and development?*
6. **Inspect** to self-assess	Draw conclusions and include more formative statements. *Does the artifact say what I want it to say about me?*
7. **Perfect** and evaluate	Refine selections and include evaluative statements. *What else could I say about this artifact that would give a better demonstration of my competence?*
8. **Inject/Eject** to update	Maintain currency in reflections. *Is this the best example of my performance on the standard? If not, what could I replace it with?*
9. **Connect** and collaborate	Conduct meaningful dialogue with others through reflections. *Whom could I get more feedback from regarding my portfolio?*
10. **Respect** accomplishments	Celebrate, display, and incorporate summative statements. (Process repeats.) *What finishing touches can I add to help the portfolio speak for itself?*

SOURCE: Adapted from Barrett (2000), *Electronic Portfolios = Multimedia Development + Portfolio Development*. Retrieved from http://electronicportfolios.org/portfolios/EPDevProcess.html.

Table 3.4 Ten Categories of Reflective Practice in Action Research

Category 1	Setting Clear Goals
Category 2	Assessing the Situation
Category 3	Creating Action Strategies
Category 4	Implementing Action Strategies
Category 5	Monitoring One's Own Actions
Category 6	Assessing Others' Reactions
Category 7	Evaluating What Others Have Learned
Category 8	Confronting Oneself With the Results
Category 9	Reflecting on What to Do Next
Category 10	Setting New Goals

SOURCE: Adapted from Schmuck (1997), *Practical Action Research for Change.* Thousand Oaks, CA: Corwin. Chapter 1, p. 16. Reprinted with permission of Corwin Press, Inc.

Pennsylvania Assessment Through Themes (PATT, 2000) offers a list of prompts, which can be used to guide candidates in formulating their reflections. These are summarized in Table 3.6.

Scheduling Reflections in the Portfolio Process

Reflections become more meaningful and manageable when they are scheduled and integrated into the entire portfolio process. One way of scheduling reflections is to include them as part of assignments or regular course activities. For example, candidates can be asked to add a reflection after they have completed an assignment as part of their grade for that assignment. They can also write goal statements at the beginning of a course or program, or conclude their work with a course or program reflection statement. In some courses, candidates may be asked to provide weekly formative reflections on their activities. Or candidates might prepare an executive summary of the entire portfolio at the completion of the portfolio process. Chapter 4 offers a timeline that elaborates on scheduling intervals for including and updating portfolio reflections. Tables 3.7 and 3.8 give samples of prompts

Table 3.5 The Multifaceted, Cyclical Nature of Portfolio Reflection

Category 1. Setting Clear Goals **Projection:** Defining a purpose for the portfolio **Guiding Questions:** How can a portfolio best serve me? What type or types of portfolio should I develop and why?	**Category 6.** Assessing Others' Reactions **Connection:** Collaboration with others **Guiding Questions:** What conclusions, adjustments, or revisions are suggested through my collaborations with others? Whom should I collaborate with and why?
Category 2. Assessing the Situation **Collection** of artifacts **Guiding Questions:** What artifacts will I collect and why? What types of reflections will I include on each artifact? How do artifacts demonstrate program goals and standards?	**Category 7.** Evaluating What Others Have Learned **Inspection:** Drawing conclusions based on reactions of others **Guiding Questions:** What conclusions can I draw from what others have learned from me? How can I benefit from these conclusions?
Category 3. Creating Action Strategies **Selection** of artifacts, prioritizing, and organizing **Guiding Questions:** What artifacts best present my competencies and skills? Which artifacts are consistent with my portfolio purpose?	**Category 8.** Confronting Oneself With the Results **Perfecting/Respecting:** Refining and celebrating one's accomplishments **Guiding Questions:** What do these results tell me about myself and my practice in relation to my goals? How do I use these results to refine my portfolio and my practice? What strengths can I highlight as a result?
Category 4. Implementing Action Strategies **Interjection** of style and organization to emphasize purpose and type of portfolio	**Category 9.** Reflecting on What to Do Next **Injection/Ejection** of artifacts to update perfecting, refining, and modifying of portfolio

Guiding Questions: What tone do I want the portfolio to have? What media will I use to give tone and style?	**Guiding Questions:** How do I modify my artifacts to better demonstrate my goals? How do I refine my portfolio (purpose)?
Category 5. Monitoring One's Own Actions **Reflection:** Formative assessment of progress **Guiding Questions:** How do I measure up to the standards and criteria? What am I learning about my practice/implementation? How do I document my growth?	**Category 10.** Setting New Goals **Projection:** Retooling portfolio and defining new purpose and goals **Guiding Questions:** What new goals and directions do I want for the portfolio? Where do I go from here professionally? What are my next steps?

SOURCE: Reflective terms adapted from Barrett (2000), p. 3.

that can be used for weekly course reflections and end-of-course reflections. The actual scheduling of reflections is left largely up to the instructors' and candidates' discretion.

Levels of Reflection in the Portfolio Process: A Sample Rubric

How does one measure levels of reflection in portfolio development? How much reflection should be included, and how do reflections influence the overall effectiveness of the portfolio? Questions such as these are common both to credential candidates who are developing their own professional portfolios and to instructors who are guiding them through the process. This section is devoted to the portfolio process of outlining criteria for assessing levels of reflection and reflective inquiry.

Whether one is preparing a traditional, two-dimensional portfolio or a multidimensional electronic portfolio (described in Chapter 7), lack of reflections has the same debilitating impact, rendering the portfolio ineffective and ambiguous. Table 3.9, adapted from Barrett (2001), serves as a type of scoring rubric for candidates and evaluators of professional portfolios to

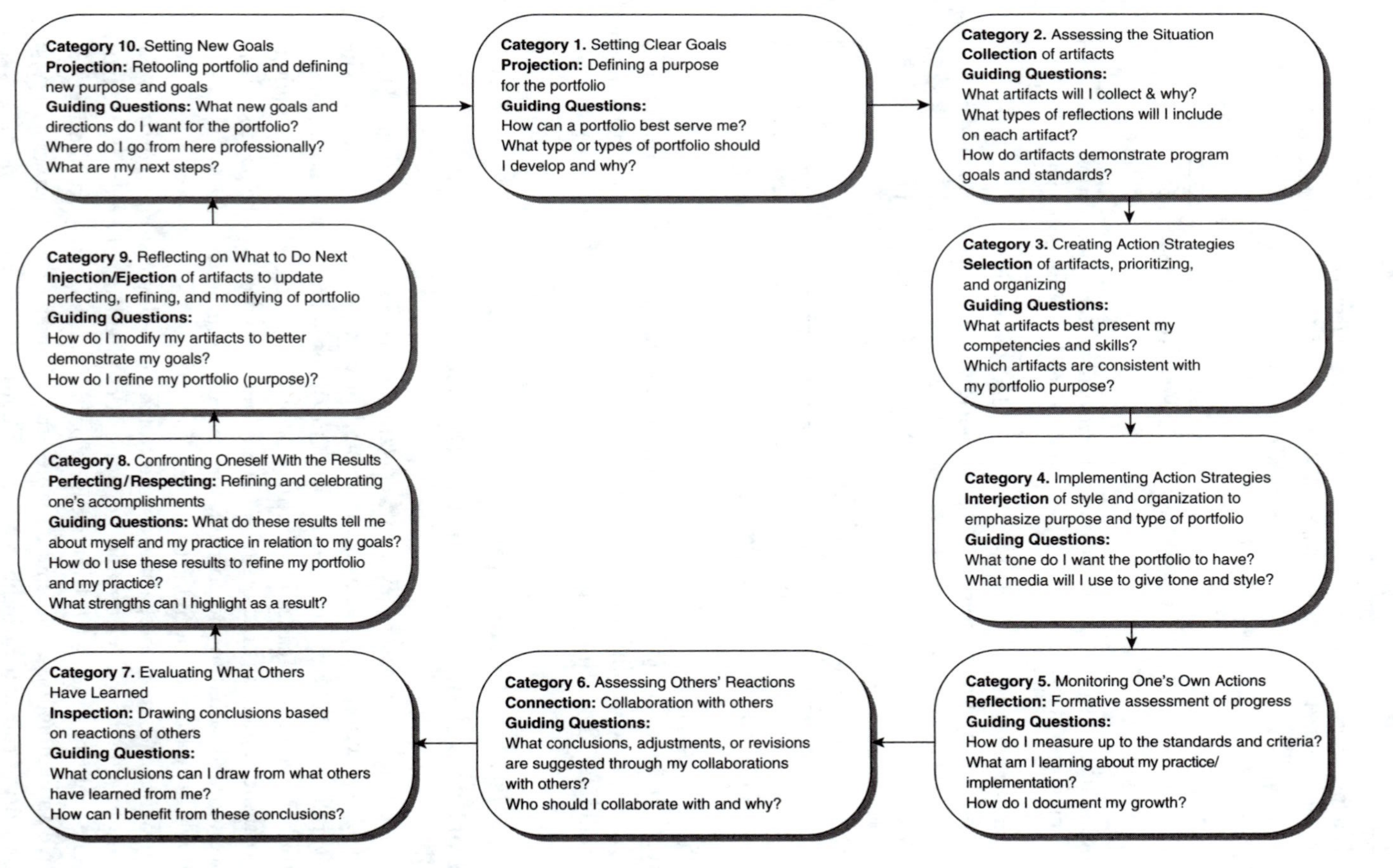
Category 1. Setting Clear Goals
Projection: Defining a purpose for the portfolio
Guiding Questions:
How can a portfolio best serve me?
What type or types of portfolio should I develop and why?
Category 2. Assessing the Situation
Collection of artifacts
Guiding Questions:
What artifacts will I collect & why?
What types of reflections will I include on each artifact?
How do artifacts demonstrate program goals and standards?
Category 3. Creating Action Strategies
Selection of artifacts, prioritizing, and organizing
Guiding Questions:
What artifacts best present my competencies and skills?
Which artifacts are consistent with my portfolio purpose?
Category 4. Implementing Action Strategies
Interjection of style and organization to emphasize purpose and type of portfolio
Guiding Questions:
What tone do I want the portfolio to have?
What media will I use to give tone and style?
Category 5. Monitoring One's Own Actions
Reflection: Formative assessment of progress
Guiding Questions:
How do I measure up to the standards and criteria?
What am I learning about my practice/implementation?
How do I document my growth?
Category 6. Assessing Others' Reactions
Connection: Collaboration with others
Guiding Questions:
What conclusions, adjustments, or revisions are suggested through my collaborations with others?
Who should I collaborate with and why?
Category 7. Evaluating What Others Have Learned
Inspection: Drawing conclusions based on reactions of others
Guiding Questions:
What conclusions can I draw from what others have learned from me?
How can I benefit from these conclusions?
Category 8. Confronting Oneself With the Results
Perfecting/Respecting: Refining and celebrating one's accomplishments
Guiding Questions: What do these results tell me about myself and my practice in relation to my goals?
How do I use these results to refine my portfolio and my practice?
What strengths can I highlight as a result?
Category 9. Reflecting on What to Do Next
Injection/Ejection of artifacts to update perfecting, refining, and modifying of portfolio
Guiding Questions:
How do I modify my artifacts to better demonstrate my goals?
How do I refine my portfolio (purpose)?
Category 10. Setting New Goals
Projection: Retooling portfolio and defining new purpose and goals
Guiding Questions: What new goals and directions do I want for the portfolio?
Where do I go from here professionally?
What are my next steps?

Figure 3.1 The Multifaceted, Cyclical Nature of Portfolio Reflection

Table 3.6 Prompts for Candidates' Self-Reflection

1. Reflection • I have chosen to include this work sample because . . . • If I did this assignment over, I would . . . because . . . • Completing this portfolio reflection has helped me increase my knowledge and understanding of . . . because . . .
2. Collaboration (for a group activity) • My role in the activity was . . . • I would give the group a grade of . . . for the activity because . . . • I would give myself a grade of . . . because . . . • I might change the way the group worked together because . . .
3. Understanding • I now know . . . about the topic that I didn't know before. • A summary of the information about the topic in this work entry would be . . . • Examples of accurate information and ideas about this work entry would be . . . • Examples of the connections among different ideas in this work entry would be . . . • Examples of the patterns and trends discussed in this work entry would be . . .
4. Inquiry • The next step of problem solving I would do is . . . because . . . • If I could do more research/study/experimentation (circle one) about this entry, I would choose to . . . because . . . • Other questions about this topic that have occurred to me are . . .
5. Communication • I focused and organized the information in this work entry in the following ways: . . . • I expressed the information in this work entry clearly by . . .
6. Personal Relevance • What I liked most/least about this topic was . . . because . . . • I can apply this knowledge/understanding in my daily life by . . . • I can apply this knowledge/understanding to the controversies/issues of . . . because . . . • This topic is interesting to me because . . . • I explained how this topic is connected to other topics in these ways: . . . • I explained the different choices people have about this topic in these ways: . . .

SOURCE: Adapted from Pennsylvania Assessment Through Themes (PATT, 2000).

Table 3.7 Sample Prompts for Weekly Course Reflections

In writing your reflections, you may want to consider some or all of the suggestions below. You are by no means limited to these items. Please expand on these suggestions or include other thoughts and comments.

1. What has changed for you?
   - Perceptions—changed or reinforced
   - Deeper learning
   - New quandaries
2. What were this week's most powerful learning experiences?
3. Have your perceptions changed in any way?
4. What areas will you continue to develop?
5. Will you revise your vision as a result of something you learned or experienced? How?

Table 3.8 Sample Prompts for End-of-Course Reflections

In writing your reflections, you may want to consider some or all of the suggestions below. You are by no means limited to these items. Please expand on these suggestions or include other thoughts and comments. It would be helpful for you to reflect on your assignments and to review the course outline and your weekly reflections to refresh your memory about some of the topics covered in earlier class sessions.

1. What has changed for you?
   - Perceptions—changed or reinforced
   - Deeper learning
   - New quandaries
2. What were some of the most powerful learning experiences?
3. Have your perceptions about teaching (leadership, counseling) changed in any way?
4. What areas will you continue to develop?
5. Will you revise your vision as a result of this course? How?

indicate how reflections should be used to strengthen and clarify the purpose of the portfolio. The table shows levels of reflection and sample artifacts in the portfolio process by including a range from Level 0, where little or no reflection is included, to Level 5, where extensive reflection is incorporated throughout.

The descriptions below are an expanded explanation of the levels in Table 3.9.

Portfolios at Level 0 include no reflections and are viewed as highly ineffective scrapbooks.

Portfolios at Level 1 include only an introductory reflection stating the purpose of the portfolio or a summative reflection at the end of the portfolio. These could be general statements about the overall portfolio process or summary statements about the cumulative nature of the artifacts.

At Level 2, along with an overall portfolio reflection, curriculum standards and portfolio goals are indicated. In this way, the artifacts are provided as evidence of meeting standards or accomplishing goals. These types of reflections would be vital in assessment and learning portfolios to measure growth and accomplishments toward those goals.

Building upon Level 2, at Level 3, reflections could include explanations of how the standards or goals were met, strategies used to accomplish these goals, and what was learned through the process. In addition, Level 3 reflections indicate future goals and projections for education, professional development, or career advancement. These types of reflections are valuable in all three types of portfolios, whether learning/working portfolios, assessment portfolios, or showcase/employment portfolios.

Level 4 contains additional reflections for each artifact in terms of explaining its purpose and reason for being included. A sample could be an award from a particular service organization, such as the Rotary Club commending the candidate for creating a "Grandparents & Books" program at various community centers. In the reflection, the candidate could indicate goals and standards that were met as a result of the award, but the candidate may also include pictures of other community events nationally and internationally, demonstrating an ongoing commitment to service learning and community outreach through the reflections on these artifacts.

Level 5 relies on the addition of connecting statements that give evidence of collaborative reflections gathered through sharing the portfolio with a variety of audiences. These types of reflections provide the strongest evidence of using the portfolio in the context of a learning community. The process thus incorporates feedback from multiple sources to strengthen the portfolio and to support the candidate's professional development. Another asset to Level 5 reflections is the self-evaluation statement from the candidate. This indicates what has been learned through

Table 3.9 Levels of Reflection and Reflective Inquiry in the Portfolio Process

0	*1*	*2*	*3*	*4*	*5*
Little or no reflection or mention of standards or goals. A collection of artifacts, a scrapbook, or multimedia presentation	Simple overall reflection on the portfolio as a whole. A general summative statement	Level 1 PLUS standards or portfolio goals are included	Level 2 PLUS reflections on achieving each standard or goal PLUS future directions (learning goals)	Level 3 PLUS reflections on role of each artifact in the portfolio	Level 4 PLUS feedback from portfolio conferencing and responses from others. Includes self-evaluation of portfolio
Sample artifact: Pictures	Sample artifact: Course portfolio I completed at the end of my first field assignment	Sample artifact: Parent letter to demonstrate INTASC Principle 10	Sample artifact: Parent letter: I plan to use a variety of letters and home links in my lessons to ensure ongoing parental involvement. I will also survey my parents for additional feedback	Sample artifact: Opening statement: This portfolio is organized according to each INTASC principle. Items in each section provide evidence of my fulfillment of the principle	Sample artifact: Letter from university supervisor along with supporting completed portfolio rubric

SOURCE: Helen Barrett (2000), hbarrett@uaa.alaska.edu. Adapted from Barrett (2000), *Electronic Portfolios = Multimedia Development + Portfolio Development*. Retrieved from http://electronicportfolios.org/portfolios/EPDevProcess.html p. 7.

the portfolio process and how the candidate has benefited. Level 5 portfolio reflections thus incorporate all of the types and aspects of reflections and reflective inquiry and therefore are viewed as the most effective and advantageous type of portfolio. Reflections at Level 5 are also beneficial and appropriate for inclusion in all three types of portfolios because they provide such comprehensive types of information about the artifacts and their overall role in the portfolio. These types of reflections offer the candidate the greatest flexibility in "retooling" and refining the portfolio for future purposes.

Outcomes and Benefits of Reflection and Reflective Inquiry

In this final section, we return to our original questions: What is the value of reflection and reflective inquiry in the portfolio process? Why include reflections? Are these really necessary?

The primary outcomes of reflective inquiry in portfolio development are an increase in *self-esteem,* resulting from recording and reflecting on achievements and successes, as well as *professional renewal* through the process of mapping new goals and planning for future growth. These benefits are true for both individual candidates and program instructors. Just as candidates can see how they have progressed systematically toward their goals, program instructors can determine what candidates are learning from their program and if program goals are being met. Another benefit is that reflections establish an *ongoing dialogue* between candidates and instructors, particularly when they include Level 5 reflections.

Summary

This chapter points out the importance of reflections and reflective inquiry in the portfolio process as setting a foundation for the portfolio and aligning it to a specific purpose. Candidates can enter a program with a clear idea of how the course activities help fulfill the standards outlined in the program, and what outcomes in the course can later become critical artifacts in the candidates' portfolio. Reflections are the products used to give voice to each artifact, and reflective inquiry is the action research process of using guiding questions in the collection and documentation of artifacts. A variety of strategies produce useful reflections that help shape the portfolio and make it a more effective tool for professional growth and planning. The next chapter discusses the process of organizing the portfolio so that its value becomes even more transparent. Other, more practical, strategies are also presented.

For Further Reading

Campbell, V. M., Cignetti, P. B., Melenyzer, B. J., Nettles, D. H., & Wyman, R. M., Jr. (2004). *How to develop a professional portfolio: A manual for teachers* (3rd ed.). Boston: Allyn & Bacon.

Rieman, P. (2000). *Teaching portfolios: Presenting your professional best.* Boston: McGraw-Hill.

Additional rubrics for assessing and evaluating portfolios are provided on the CD.

PART II

A Guide on Developing Portfolios

4

Organizing and Implementing the Portfolio

A Developmental Process

A well-designed portfolio assessment process evaluates the effectiveness of your intervention at the same time that it evaluates the growth of individuals or communities. It also serves as a communication tool.

—Sewell, Marczak, & Horn (2000), *The Use of Portfolio Assessment in Evaluation*

Chapter Objectives

Readers will be able to

- discuss the implementation of the portfolio process,
- describe the major phases of program organization,
- set timelines and benchmarks in the portfolio process,
- use standards and performance assessment in portfolio evaluation and scoring,
- discuss the potential pitfalls of the developmental process and how to address them.

Scenario

It was easy to hear the frustration in Marga's voice as she shared her reflections on the portfolio process during her final presentation session as a teaching credential candidate at Sunshine University. She began, "In the end, I could see that the portfolio was a good thing, but it bothered me that I really could not see it as a good thing until the very end of our program, and . . . then it was too late!" Marga continued, "We heard only a few comments about needing a portfolio at the beginning of the program, during the Introduction to Teaching course, and then, again, at the very end, when we were supposed to turn it in. Most of our professors said nothing about it or about which assignments would make good artifacts. Had I known then what I know now, it would have been so much easier to build my portfolio because I would have saved more items from the courses and the program. At first, I did not understand how the assignments were related to the standards. I knew about the K–12 subject matter standards we were supposed to be teaching our elementary and secondary students, but little was said about the teaching standards and how the courses were helping us to meet them as a teacher. It did not come together for me until the Student Teaching Seminar, when we got a full outline of the teaching standards and the recommended portfolio table of contents. It finally all started to make sense. It would have been nice to hear about the portfolio from each of our professors and how their assignments addressed the various standards. Now I can see that the courses did address the standards, but that was not always made explicit to the students."

Several other credential candidates chimed in and nodded heads in agreement. "I threw away so much stuff once the class was over and I got the grade," commented Julio, another credential candidate, in agreement. "Now that I look at the standard, I realize that it wasn't always the final grade in the class but the process I went through in the class that was most important. The portfolio helps you identify and articulate that process. It's real hard to go back and collect or re-create those pieces at the end! I think it would help if our professors talked to each other about the process and each mentioned the portfolio as it relates to their course and the overall credential program. That would be a big support for the students!"

"You took the words right out of my mouth," declared Larry, another credential candidate. "What helped me in preparing my portfolio was my Master Teacher sharing her portfolio with me from her credential program. She shared that each of her professors talked about the portfolio throughout the program. I believe professors also need to talk to each other and agree on the guidelines for what artifacts to include and how they will be evaluated."

Dr. Young, the instructor for the Student Teaching Seminar and the final portfolio presentation session, shared these comments from credential candidates with the credential program chair and education dean later that afternoon. As a result of the comments from Dr. Young and other education faculty at Sunshine University who were experiencing the same thing, portfolio guidelines were added to each course, along with suggestions for which assignments to include and how those assignments addressed specific teaching standards. Dialogues also began among all faculty members in the credential program regarding new strategies they could each incorporate to support the candidates throughout the portfolio process.

Overview

As the scenario suggests, the portfolio is not simply a collection of artifacts to be turned in at the completion of a program, but rather a dynamic process of planning, reflecting, collecting, and evaluating that occurs throughout the entire program and, ideally, extends throughout one's career. The purpose of this chapter is to lay out a blueprint for making the portfolio process meaningful and informative throughout the credential program for both students and instructors. Specific strategies are presented for effectively managing and implementing the portfolio process. The chapter begins with a brief description of the major phases of the portfolio process and general program organization. Potential pitfalls of the portfolio process and ways to address them follow. The chapter continues with recommendations for setting timelines and benchmarks for both instructors and candidates, which is meant to support them in meeting the time management challenges inherent in portfolio development. Next, descriptions of using standards in setting criteria for effective portfolio assessment are followed by recommendations for enhancing the portfolio scoring process. The chapter concludes with strategies for promoting continuous program renewal and evaluation through portfolios.

Implementation Design for the Portfolio Process

A multitude of literature supports the importance of having a specific design for the portfolio implementation process (Barrett, 2000; Forgette-Giroux & Simon, 2000; Pennsylvania Assessment Through Themes, 2000; Wilkerson & Lang, 2003). In this chapter, several suggestions and recommendations are made; however, programs need to tailor the process to their specific needs. For the portfolio to be most effective as a tool for authentic assessment and evaluation, careful consideration must be given to clear articulation of a process or implementation plan that is designed and agreed upon by all stakeholders (Wilkerson & Lang, 2003).

One of the most challenging aspects for all participants involved in the portfolio process is managing the time it takes to develop a quality portfolio. Designing a strategic plan for portfolio implementation is one way to address the time challenges. Forgette-Giroux and Simon (2000) suggested that the portfolio process involves four types of organizational issues: temporal, spatial, human, and contextual. Temporal issues concern time spent on planning and scheduling portfolio assessment-related activities and their place within existing teaching and assessment practices. Spatial issues deal with organizing the portfolio's format, design, and physical characteristics; storage; and access. Human issues include role-sharing responsibilities such as establishing and updating a table of contents, dating and sorting portfolio entries, reflection, and marking and scoring for formative or summative evaluation purposes. Last, contextual aspects have to do with specifying the object of assessment, identifying the standards, determining the scope of disciplines from which portfolio artifacts are selected, and establishing criteria for their quantity and quality.

Major Phases of Portfolio Organization

Barrett (2000) identified five major phases of portfolio development or organization: *collection, selection, reflection, projection,* and *presentation* (see Table 4.1 for more detail). These phases build on earlier discussions of reflections in the portfolio process, discussed in Chapter 3, and using portfolios as authentic assessment, discussed in Chapter 2. In addition, they reinforce the importance of numerous discussions at each phase, involving all stakeholders in terms of clarifying and refining the process.

Table 4.1 is a modification that has been made to Barrett's (2000) original table, with the inclusion of *projection* as both a beginning phase and a follow-up phase in the process. This reinforces the vital role of goal setting, planning, and reflection throughout the portfolio process. It also emphasizes the cyclical nature of portfolio development, in that each phase supports and helps to define the next. It is important to begin the process with projection and to keep projection as a major step that candidates and instructors return to throughout the portfolio process. Before even starting to collect artifacts, it is imperative to "begin with the end in mind" (Covey, 1990). This is true for individuals as well as for programs. Candidates and instructors must set

Table 4.1 Phases of the Portfolio Development Process

Projection	Candidates and instructors decide on the purpose(s) for the portfolio and the role it will play in the program (e.g., formative assessment, summative evaluation). The desired context for the portfolio is set. Preliminary planning begins for addressing temporal, spatial, and human issues.
Collection	Candidates and instructors save artifacts that represent achievement of specific standards and "growth opportunities." The portfolio's purpose and audience will determine what is collected at this stage.
Selection	Candidates and instructors review and evaluate the artifacts they have saved, and they identify those that best demonstrate achievement of specific standards. The selection criteria should reflect the learning objectives of the portfolio.
Reflection	Candidates and instructors articulate their thinking about each piece in their portfolio, evaluating their own growth over time and their achievement of the standards. It is recommended to include reflections on each piece, plus an overall reflection on the entire portfolio.
Projection	Candidates and instructors compare their reflections with the standards and performance indicators and set future learning goals. This phase transforms portfolio development into professional development, not only for the individual but also for the program.
Connection/ Presentation	Candidates and instructors share portfolios with the appropriate audience, including their peers and supervisors, and collaborate on the contents, process, and purpose of portfolios. The feedback at this stage can lead to "public" commitments of professional development and future goal setting.

SOURCE: Adapted from Barrett (2000).

a purpose for the portfolio and describe how they envision the portfolio process will serve both the individual and the program. All stakeholders in the portfolio process must be made aware of the multiple purposes that the portfolio can serve in both formative and summative evaluation of programs, as well as of individuals, as mentioned in Chapter 2. With those purposes in mind, candidates can begin refining the types of materials they will collect, being sure to give attention to temporal, spatial, human, and contextual issues.

Table 4.2 presents some questions to keep in mind at each phase of the portfolio process; the questions also address temporal, spatial, human, and contextual issues. These types of questions are valuable for both candidates and program instructors in planning and implementing the portfolio process; in an identified program, they provide a comprehensive overview of the major issues involved. The questions can further serve as planning guidelines for which specific people and types of activities are appropriate at each stage. Many of these questions should be discussed and agreed upon among the stakeholders at various points of the process to ensure clarity, understanding, and "buy-in." For new programs, these questions should be reviewed and discussed in their entirety as a major step in planning and development among program instructors. If possible, they should also be reviewed by potential candidates to help in establishing program and portfolio guidelines simultaneously. The answers to these questions, in turn, become the blueprint and framework for the portfolio process in the specific program under consideration.

There are several other recommendations to facilitate the management and organization of the portfolio implementation process. Although some ideas are more appropriate for program instructors, both the instructors and candidates will benefit from an ongoing dialogue regarding portfolio implementation. Pennsylvania Assessment Through Themes (PATT, 2000) outlined numerous strategies for this process in Tables 4.3 and 4.4.

Potential Pitfalls of the Portfolio Process and How to Address Them

As previously mentioned, the two major potential pitfalls of the portfolio process are (1) time management and (2) portfolio scoring. Both can be effectively addressed if they are integrated into the process as fundamental steps that are developed and agreed upon by all stakeholders during the early planning stages. Portfolio timelines and scoring should also be revisited and modified throughout the process, based on feedback from program instructors and candidates during regular intervals in the program. The following two sections lay out specific recommendations for taking a proactive approach with time management and the scoring of portfolios.

Table 4.2 Questions for Each Phase of Portfolio Development

Phase	Questions
Projection	**Contextual** • What purposes do I want the portfolio to serve? • What competencies do I want/need to demonstrate, and what criteria will I use to assess them? **Temporal** • What is a reasonable amount of time to allow for this process? **Spatial** • What form is best for storage and retrieval of artifacts? • What strategies can be used for managing and organizing artifacts and reflections? **Human** • Who should be involved in the process, and how and when should they become involved?
Collection	**Contextual** • What artifacts represent achievement of specific standards and "growth opportunities"? • How do I reference each artifact (e.g., labels, reflections)? **Temporal** • When do I begin to collect, and for how long should I collect? **Spatial** • What form is best for storage and retrieval of artifacts? **Human** • Who should be involved in the collection of artifacts? • Who can support in the collection of artifacts, and in what ways?
Selection	**Contextual** • What artifacts best represent achievement of specific standards and "growth opportunities"? **Temporal** • When do I begin to refine my selections, and for how long? **Spatial** • What form is best for ranking and separating artifacts during storage and retrieval (e.g., manila folders, color coding, file cabinet, sticky notes, reflections)? **Human** • Who should be involved in the selection and evaluation of artifacts? • Who can support in the selection and evaluation of artifacts, and in what ways? • Who should be involved in establishing and reviewing criteria?

<table>
<tr><td>Reflection</td><td>Contextual
• What types of reflections best articulate thinking regarding each artifact and its role in evaluating growth over time and in achievement of the standards?

Temporal
• When is the best time to add reflections, and how do I schedule time for regularly adding and reviewing artifacts and reflections?

Spatial
• What form is best for storage and retrieval of reflections?
• Where should I add reflections to the artifacts?

Human
• Who can provide support and give feedback on the artifacts and reflections?
• What strategies can help with the storage and retrieval of reflections on a regular basis (e.g., sticky notes, index cards)?</td></tr>
<tr><td>Projection</td><td>Contextual
• When artifacts and reflections are compared with standards and performance indicators, what future learning goals can be set?

Temporal
• Is the timeline appropriate for reaching the desired benchmarks, or should adjustments be made in future planning?
• Have appropriate timelines and benchmarks been set for the program, and what adjustments should be made, if any, in looking toward the future?

Spatial
• Are the storage and retrieval systems adequate for demonstrating growth over time and achievement when compared with the standards and performance indicators, or should modifications be made for future enhancement?

Human
• Who can support in comparing artifacts and reflections with the standards and for setting future learning goals?
• When can and should this type of collaboration be scheduled?</td></tr>
<tr><td>Connection/ Presentation</td><td>Contextual
• Is the overall purpose of the portfolio clear to my audience?</td></tr>
</table>

(Continued)

Table 4.2 (Continued)

	Temporal • What is the best format for the presentation, given the time limitations? **Spatial** • What is the best format for the presentation, given the space limitations? **Human** • Who is the appropriate audience (e.g., peers, supervisors) for sharing the portfolio and collaborating on its contents, process, and purpose? • What is the best format for the portfolio presentation, given the specific purpose and the specific audience?

SOURCE: Based on terms from Barrett (2000).

Table 4.3 Portfolio Management Ideas

1. Set up a timeline with due dates for installments.
   - Provide ample time to review and comment on the progress.
   - Make reflection sheets available for practice runs and provide ongoing guidance.
   - Have candidates practice writing reflective statements for each potential portfolio entry.

2. Provide samples of completed portfolios and emphasize the importance of appearance in the scoring (e.g., organization, table of contents, use of graphics).
   - Encourage the incorporation of technology, such as electronic portfolios (see Chapter 7).

3. To ensure clarity of expectations and scoring, present the rubrics or scoring guides in advance.
   - Encourage candidates to practice self- and peer scoring of projects and the portfolio itself, such as oral or written comments to each other.

4. Make the portfolio process convenient!
   - Use materials that are readily available, such as manila folders, sticky notes, and storage boxes.

- Store folders, alphabetically, in milk crates, cardboard boxes, or file cabinets.
- Use binders equipped with a space for video- or audiocassettes.
- Color code to distinguish among classes, or use a different file drawer.
- Actively engage candidates in the management of the portfolio system and establish regular classroom portfolio sessions.

SOURCE: Adapted from PATT (2000).

Table 4.4 Tips for Keeping a Portfolio

1. Always place a table of contents with dates and page numbers at or near the front.
2. Keep work for each unit or course in a folder, and then select a certain number of pieces at the end of the quarter or semester.
3. Photocopy and/or keep electronic files of group work so that members can include the work in their portfolios.
4. Include the instructor prompt with each work entered.
5. Photograph or scan work that is too cumbersome to fit into the folder.
6. Tape (audio or video) students' explanations or oral presentations.
7. Keep computer disks or printouts of relevant material.
8. Include photographs of pre-K–12 students carrying out their work (e.g., an experiment or a group activity).

SOURCE: Adapted from PATT (2000).

Setting Timelines and Benchmarks in the Portfolio Process

Time management has been emphasized as one of the most critical elements in portfolio implementation (Barrett, 2000; Campbell, Cignetti, Melenyzer, Nettles, & Wyman, 2004; PATT, 2000). Establishing timelines with clearly defined benchmarks allows program instructors and candidates to schedule activities and pace themselves in completing the portfolio in a timely manner. The challenge is to identify relevant activities scheduled at appropriate intervals of time. This should be done throughout a program but also throughout each course in the program to provide continuity and consistency of information. Parameters of the timelines and benchmarks need to be discussed and agreed upon by program instructors; in this way, each instructor in the program has ownership of the portfolio process and plays a pivotal role in pacing the candidates. In specific programs, such as those leading to a teaching, administrative, or counseling credential, important time intervals come at the beginning of the program, midway through the program, at the end of the program, and at natural breaks in the program, usually marked by semesters, quarters, or courses.

Two samples of program portfolio timelines are presented in Table 4.5 and Table 4.6, which identify portfolio benchmarks that correspond to a candidate's time in the program. Table 4.5 has ten suggested checkpoints that are appropriate for longer programs lasting two or more years. Table 4.6 has five suggested checkpoints that are appropriate for shorter programs lasting a year or less. Please note, however, that the checkpoints listed on Table 4.5 and Table 4.6 are only general indicators of the types of activities that facilitate pacing of the portfolio process. Specific checkpoints and activities should be adapted for each program, and the appropriate timelines and benchmarks should be developed after stakeholders have collaborated and agreed on them.

There should be a continuous process of verification of completion of competencies throughout the program. This documentation will be critical for summative evaluations. Each candidate will need to keep a record of the certification of competencies. Programs should develop a template or checklist that candidates will use. It is also recommended that candidates continue to reflect on their portfolios even after the completion of their programs and use the portfolios to guide future areas for professional development or employment opportunities. This is described as an ongoing checkpoint that continues after the completion of the program, course, or workshop. This process will be addressed more in Chapter 8, which discusses keeping the portfolio alive.

Portfolios can also be developed within a particular course or workshop as a way of helping candidates to organize and systematically collect artifacts that document growth and progress toward course or workshop goals and objectives. The portfolios may also include standards as criteria for meeting course goals. These types of portfolios are often referred to as *developmental, academic,* or *working* portfolios, as described in Chapter 1. In some cases, as in mini-courses leading to certification in a particular skill or competency, such as designing programs for special populations (e.g., Inquiry Approaches to Science and Social Studies for English Language Learners, or Building a Comprehensive Partnership With Parents and Community, or Steps to Opening Your Own Charter School), developing and maintaining a

Table 4.5 Sample Program Portfolio Checkpoint Timeline—Longer Programs (Two or More Years)

Timeline/ Time Interval	*Benchmark/Activity*	*Date*
Opening of Program (Checkpoint 1)	• Introduce portfolio, standards, and scoring guide to the candidates • Define portfolio terminology and show sample portfolios • Explain and provide examples of artifacts and reflections • Distribute portfolio rubric and standards to candidates • Discuss the parameters and give examples for each one • Provide portfolio timeline and benchmarks	
(Checkpoint 2)	• Further explain and define types of artifacts and reflections, showing examples of each • Have candidates complete a portfolio entry reflection for an assignment as an entire class • Have candidates draft a goal statement for the portfolio • Encourage candidates to organize a system for collecting assignments and artifacts around each targeted standard	
(Checkpoint 3)	• Review the rubric with candidates, using related assignments and activities • Require written reflections as part of some assignments • Have candidates revisit program goals and standards and project goals for next time interval • Have candidates refine goal statements and ensure that each artifact has reflections, captions, etc. • Facilitate informal portfolio exchanges and discussions among candidates, peers, mentors, and program instructors • Score portfolio standards and artifacts at each checkpoint • Instructors certify competency in standards	

(Continued)

Table 4.5 (Continued)

Timeline/ Time Interval	*Benchmark/Activity*	*Date*
(Checkpoint 4)	• Continue to align assignments to program standards and recommend as potential artifacts in portfolio • Continue to review artifact and reflection types along with rubric parameters • Conduct reflective discussions on assignments	
Midway (Checkpoint 5)	• Candidates are now halfway through the program! • Candidates should have addressed at least half of the program goals/standards with samples of artifacts and reflections for each • Have candidates to reflect on initial program goals and set goals for remainder of program • Have students share portfolios with peers/mentors for formative feedback and further goal setting • Require scoring of newly completed portfolio standards and artifacts at each checkpoint • Revisit vision and philosophy; rework if necessary • Check for instructors' sign-off on competencies	
(Checkpoint 6)	• Continue to complete assignments focused on the remainder of the program standards and goals • Revisit the portfolio rubric and contents of the portfolio, noting any gaps or missing data • Continue to update selections and reflections on portfolio entries	
(Checkpoint 7)	• Continue to complete assignments focused on the remainder of the program standards and goals • Revisit the portfolio rubric and contents of the portfolio, noting any gaps or missing data	

Timeline/ Time Interval	*Benchmark/Activity*	*Date*
	• Continue to update selections and reflections on portfolio entries • Continue scoring of newly completed portfolio standards and artifacts • Conduct informal portfolio exchanges and discussions, including reflective statements, among candidates, peers, mentors, and program instructors	
(Checkpoint 8)	• Have candidates begin an initial showcase portfolio and differentiate it from the working portfolio • Candidates can select specific artifacts and reflections for the showcase portfolio, including examples of growth and development toward the program goals and standards • Continue to review artifact and reflection types along with rubric parameters • Facilitate reflective discussions on assignments • Check for instructors' sign-off on competencies	
(Checkpoint 9)	• Have candidates to reflect on initial program goals and set goals for remainder of program • Have the candidates complete an executive portfolio summary for the individual portfolio • Revisit vision and philosophy; rework if necessary • Share portfolios with peers and mentors for formative feedback and further goal setting before final summative portfolio evaluation • Continue scoring of newly completed portfolio standards and artifacts	
End (Checkpoint 10)	• Check for instructors' sign-off on competencies • Present completed showcase portfolio to program instructors and peers as summative evaluation of candidate and program	

(Continued)

Table 4.5 (Continued)

Timeline/ Time Interval	*Benchmark/Activity*	*Date*
	• Present completed showcase portfolio to potential employers as evidence of desired competencies for targeted professional positions • Congratulations! Candidates have completed a successful portfolio process	
(Ongoing Checkpoint)	• Continue to update selections and reflections on portfolio entries • Share portfolios with peers and mentors for formative feedback and further goal setting beyond program • Facilitate informal portfolio exchanges and discussions among candidates, peers, mentors, and program instructors • Begin retooling portfolio. Project new goals and applications for professional development and growth (see Chapter 8: Keeping the Portfolio Alive)	

SOURCE: Adapted from PATT (2000).

portfolio can be a valuable resource once the course has ended. The timeline and benchmarks are parallel, regardless of the type of program, although there may be fewer checkpoints for mini-courses (see Table 4.7, page 76).

Similarly, a course portfolio may simply include evidence of assignments and reflections from a particular course, with an overall reflection at the end of the course regarding the value of the course in the professional development of the candidate and the candidates' self-evaluation of course performance. Figure 4.1 (page 79) shows a sample course portfolio table of contents for a language-development course in a teacher credential program. Each entry is supported by a corresponding INTASC Standard. The primary focus of this course is INTASC Principle 3 (Adapting Instruction for Individual Needs).

Table 4.6 Sample Program Portfolio Checkpoint Timeline—Shorter Programs (One Year or Less)

Timeline/ Time Interval	*Benchmark/Activity*	*Date*
Opening of Program (Checkpoint 1)	• Introduce portfolio and scoring guide to the candidates • Define portfolio terminology and show a sample portfolio • Explain and provide examples of artifacts and reflections • Distribute portfolio rubric and standards to candidates • Discuss the parameters and give examples for each one • Provide portfolio timeline and benchmarks • Review the rubric with candidates, using related assignments and activities	
(Checkpoint 2)	• Have candidates draft a goal statement for portfolio • Require written reflections as part of some assignments • Candidates revisit program goals and standards and project goals for next time interval • Candidates write "end of interval" reflection • Facilitate informal portfolio exchanges and discussions, including reflective statements, among candidates, peers, mentors, and program instructors • Check for instructors' sign off on competencies	
Midway (Checkpoint 3)	• Candidates are now halfway through the program! • Candidates should have addressed at least half of the program goals/standards with samples of artifacts and reflections for each • Encourage candidates to reflect on initial program goals and set goals for remainder of program • Have candidates refine goal statements and ensure each artifact has reflections, captions, etc.	

(Continued)

Table 4.6 (Continued)

Timeline/ Time Interval	*Benchmark/Activity*	*Date*
	• Share portfolios with peers and mentors for formative feedback and further goal setting • Require scoring of newly completed portfolio standards and artifacts at each checkpoint • Revisit vision and philosophy; rework if necessary • Check for instructors' sign off on competencies	
(Checkpoint 4)	• Continue to complete assignments focused on the remainder of the program standards and goals • Revisit the portfolio rubric and contents of the portfolio, noting any gaps or missing data • Continue to update selections and reflections on portfolio entries • Facilitate informal portfolio exchanges and discussions, including reflective statements, among candidates, peers, mentors, and program instructors • Have candidates begin to differentiate the portfolio and start an initial showcase portfolio from the working portfolio • Candidates can select specific artifacts and reflections for the showcase portfolio, including examples of growth and development toward the workshop or course goals and standards • Revisit vision and philosophy; rework if necessary	
End (Checkpoint 5)	• Present completed showcase portfolio to workshop or course instructors and peers as summative evaluation of candidate and workshop or course • Present completed showcase portfolio as evidence of desired competencies for targeted areas	

Timeline/ Time Interval	*Benchmark/Activity*	*Date*
	• Candidates have completed a successful portfolio process • Check for instructors' sign off on competencies	
(Ongoing Checkpoint)	• Continue to update selections and reflections on portfolio entries • Portfolios should be shared with peers and mentors for formative feedback and further goal setting beyond program • Facilitate informal portfolio exchanges and discussions among candidates, peers, mentors, and program instructors • Begin retooling the portfolio. Project new goals and applications for professional development and growth (see Chapter 8: Keeping the Portfolio Alive)	

SOURCE: Adapted from PATT (2000).

Other sample tables of contents for portfolios are included in Chapters 5 and 7 (electronic version). The table of contents would be very similar to the course syllabus and assignments. Course and workshop portfolios are another way to expose candidates to the portfolio process when there may not be a formal portfolio process in place for the entire program. Similar benefits will still accrue in terms of inquiry, reflection, organization, and time management.

Tables 4.8, 4.9, and 4.10 (starting on page 80) provide sample checklists that can be used to document verification of introduction, development, and mastery of program competencies at various points of a teacher, administrator, or counseling credential program. As portfolios are reviewed at certain checkpoints throughout the perspective program, reviewers can indicate when the portfolio was reviewed and the level of progress toward the standard or competencies emphasized in the program. Such a checklist would also provide an overview of where and to what level specific competencies were addressed in courses. It is particularly helpful to have portfolio artifacts organized around specific standards. This is also true of assignments in

Table 4.7 Sample Course or Workshop Portfolio Timeline—Always Quality Over Quantity

Timeline/ Time Interval	*Benchmark/Activity*	*Date*
Opening of Workshop or Course (Checkpoint 1)	• Introduce portfolio and scoring guide to the candidates • Define portfolio terminology and show a sample portfolio • Explain and provide examples of artifacts and reflections • Distribute portfolio rubric and standards to candidates • Discuss the parameters and give examples for each one • Provide portfolio timeline and benchmarks	
(Checkpoint 2)	• Review the rubric with candidates using related assignments and activities • Have candidates draft a goal statement for portfolio • Encourage written reflections as part of some assignments • Candidates revisit program goals and standards and project goals for next time interval • Candidates write "end of interval" reflection • Facilitate informal portfolio exchanges and discussions, including reflective statements, among candidates, peers, mentors, and program instructors • Check for instructors' sign-off on competencies	
Midway (Checkpoint 3)	• Candidates are now halfway through the workshop or course! • Candidates should have addressed at least half of the workshop or course's goals and standards with samples of artifacts and reflections for each • Require candidates to reflect on initial workshop or course goals and set goals for remainder of workshop or course	

Timeline/ Time Interval	*Benchmark/Activity*	*Date*
	• Candidates refine goal statements and ensure each artifact has reflections, captions, etc. • Share portfolios with peers and mentors for formative feedback and further goal setting • Require scoring of newly completed portfolio standards and artifacts at each checkpoint • Check for instructors' sign-off on competencies	
(Checkpoint 4)	• Continue to complete assignments focused on the remainder of the workshop or course standards and goals • Revisit the portfolio rubric and contents of the portfolio, noting any gaps or missing data • Continue to update selections and reflections on portfolio entries • Faciliate informal portfolio exchanges and discussions, including reflective statements, among candidates, peers, mentors, and program instructors	
(Checkpoint 5)	• Check for instructors' sign-off on competencies • Have candidates begin to differentiate the portfolio and start an initial showcase portfolio from the working portfolio • Candidates can select specific artifacts and reflections for the showcase portfolio, including examples of growth and development toward the workshop or course goals and standards • Continue to review artifact and reflection types along with rubric parameters • Facilitate reflective discussions on assignments • Continue scoring of newly completed portfolio standards and artifacts	

(Continued)

Table 4.7 (Continued)

Timeline/ Time Interval	*Benchmark/Activity*	*Date*
End (Checkpoint 6)	• Present completed showcase portfolio to workshop or course instructors and peers as summative evaluation of candidate and workshop or course • Present completed showcase portfolio as evidence of desired competencies for targeted areas • Candidates have completed a successful portfolio process	

courses such as writing lesson plans or developing organizational charts. More examples of aligning artifacts and assignments to standards are discussed in Chapters 5 to 8.

Enhancing the Portfolio Scoring Process

Another potential pitfall in portfolio implementation is scoring. Some of the concerns about scoring the portfolio involve delineating the time it takes to score, setting regular intervals for scoring, and establishing specific scoring guidelines and criteria to achieve agreement and consistency in assessing and evaluating the portfolio contents. Chapter 2 discussed the value of portfolios for both formative and summative evaluation and listed recommendations for helping them to become more reliable when used for certification purposes. Many of these recommendations centered around scoring.

PATT (2000) suggested a few additional considerations for improving the portfolio scoring process. These include the use of holistic scoring (which addresses the time issue) and collaborative scoring (which addresses setting criteria and fostering agreement and consistency in scoring) as part of portfolio professional development. Interval scoring is a third technique to break down the scoring process into manageable chunks, which takes place at regular intervals or checkpoints throughout the portfolio process. Please see suggested checkpoints on Tables 4.5 and 4.6.

Name ______________________________

Date ______________________________

Portfolio Table of Contents

EDEL 405 Language Development in Elementary School

1. **Methods and Activities Presentation** (e.g., TPR, jazz chants) (15%)
   (INTASC Principle 3, Adapting Instruction for Individual Needs)

2. **Journal Entries and Reflections** (e.g., treasures, key questions, goal setting)
   (INTASC Principle 9, Professional Commitment and Responsibility)

3. **Observation and Participation Reports**
   (INTASC Principle 9, Professional Commitment and Responsibility)

4. **Thematic ELD Unit** (25%)
   (INTASC Principle 4, Multiple Instructional Strategies; ISTE NETS Technology Standards I, II, and III)

5. **Multimedia Presentation of Unit**
   (INTASC Principle 4, Multiple Instructional Strategies; ISTE NETS Technology Standards I, II, and III)

6. **Video Assignment** (5%)
   (INTASC Principle 9, Professional Commitment and Responsibility)

7. **Peer Evaluations**
   (INTASC Principle 9, Professional Commitment and Responsibility)

8. **Self-Evaluation**
   (INTASC Principle 9, Professional Commitment and Responsibility)

9. **Picture File Samples**
   (INTASC Principle 4, Multiple Instructional Strategies; ISTE NETS Technology Standards I, II, and III)

10. **WebCT/Intel® Assignments** (e.g., Internet explorations)
    (INTASC Principle 4, Multiple Instructional Strategies; ISTE NETS Technology Standards I, II, and III)

11. **Other** (e.g., bulletin boards, classroom pictures, letters to parents, student work)
    (INTASC Principle 4, Multiple Instructional Strategies; ISTE NETS Technology Standards I, II, and III)

Figure 4.1 Sample Course Portfolio Table of Contents

Table 4.8 Sample Portfolio Checklist for Teaching Credential Candidates

INTASC Principle*	*Introduced Course/Date*	*Developing Course/Date*	*Mastery Course/Date*
Principle 1 (Knowledge of Subject Matter)	EDUC 300 (9/7/05)	EDUC 302 (1/6/06)	EDUC 400 (6/15/06)
Principle 2 (Knowledge of Human Development and Learning)	EDUC 300	EDUC 301	EDUC 400
Principle 3 (Adapting Instruction for Individual Needs)	EDUC 300	EDUC 304	EDUC 403
Principle 4 (Multiple Instructional Strategies)	EDUC 300	EDUC 302	EDUC 402
Principle 5 (Classroom Motivation and Management)	EDUC 300	EDUC 301	EDUC 402
Principle 6 (Communication Skills)	EDUC 300	EDUC 315	EDUC 400
Principle 7 (Instructional Planning Skills)	EDUC 300	EDUC 302	EDUC 405
Principle 8 (Assessment of Student Learning)	EDUC 300	EDUC 301	EDUC 415
Principle 9 (Professional Commitment and Responsibility)	EDUC 300	EDUC 305	EDUC 418
Principle 10 (Partnerships)	EDUC 300	EDUC 305	EDUC 449

*Interstate New Teacher Assessment and Support Consortium (INTASC) is a consortium of more than thirty states operating under the Council of Chief State School Officers (CCSSO) that has developed standards and an assessment process for initial teacher certification (Campbell, Melenyzer, Nettles, & Wyman, 2000).

Table 4.9 Sample Portfolio Checklist for Administrative Credential Candidates

Interstate School Leaders Licensure Consortium (ISLLC): Standards for School Leaders	*Introduced Course/Date*	*Developing Course/Date*	*Mastery Course/Date*
Standard 1: A school administrator is an educational leader who promotes the success of all students by **facilitating the development, articulation, implementation, and stewardship of a vision of learning that is shared and supported by the school community**	EDAD 500	EDAD 510	EDAD 600
Standard 2: A school administrator is an educational leader who promotes the success of all students by **advocating, nurturing, and sustaining a school culture and instructional program conducive to student learning and staff professional growth**	EDAD 500	EDAD 520	EDAD 600
Standard 3: A school administrator is an educational leader who promotes the success of all students by **ensuring the management of the organization, operations, and resources for a safe, efficient, and effective learning environment**	EDAD 500	EDAD 530	EDAD 600

(Continued)

Table 4.9 (Continued)

Interstate School Leaders Licensure Consortium (ISLLC): Standards for School Leaders	*Introduced Course/Date*	*Developing Course/Date*	*Mastery Course/Date*
Standard 4: A school administrator is an educational leader who promotes the success of all students by **collaborating with families and community members, responding to diverse community interests and needs, and mobilizing community resources**	EDAD 500	EDAD 540	EDAD 600
Standard 5: A school administrator is an educational leader who promotes the success of all students by **acting with integrity, with fairness, and in an ethical manner**	EDAD 500	EDAD 550	EDAD 600
Standard 6: A school administrator is an educational leader who promotes the success of all students by **understanding, responding to, and influencing the larger political, social, economic, legal, and cultural context**	EDAD 500	EDAD 560	EDAD 600

Holistic, Collaborative, and Interval Scoring

The holistic scoring process is one strategy recommended for portfolios by PATT (2000). When using holistic scoring for a culmination/summative portfolio, it is imperative that one use a process that is reflective of the

Table 4.10 Sample Portfolio Checklist for Counseling Credential Candidates

National Standards for School Counseling Programs	*Introduced Course/Date*	*Developing Course/Date*	*Mastery Course/Date*
Academic Development			
Standard A: Students will acquire the attitudes, knowledge, and skills that contribute to effective learning in school across the life span	COUN 400	COUN 420	COUN 500
Standard B: Students will complete school with the academic preparation essential to choose from a wide range of substantial postsecondary options, such as college	COUN 400	COUN 422	COUN 500
Standard C: Students will understand the relationship of academics to the world of work and to life at home in the community	COUN 400	COUN 425	COUN 500
Career Development			
Standard A: Students will acquire the skills to investigate the world of work in relation to knowledge of self and to make informed career decisions	COUN 400	COUN 414	COUN 520
Standard B: Students will employ strategies to achieve future career success and satisfaction	COUN 400	COUN 415	COUN 520
Standard C: Students will understand the relationship among personal qualities, education and training, and the world of work	COUN 400	COUN 416	COUN 520
Personal/Social Development			
Standard A: Students will acquire the attitudes, knowledge, and interpersonal skills to help them understand and respect self and others	COUN 400	COUN 408	COUN 560
Standard B: Students will make decisions, set goals, and take necessary action to achieve goals	COUN 400	COUN 409	COUN 560
Standard C: Students will understand safety and survival skills	COUN 400	COUN 410	COUN 560

portfolio development timelines described in Tables 4.5 and 4.6. Holistic scoring, according to PATT (2000), is getting a general impression of the entire portfolio. It is not a detailed review, nor is it a checklist process or item-by-item search. Rather, an anchor assignment or examples of past portfolios (which have had each parameter or standard scored previously) are used for this scoring system. A more detailed process for scoring specific standards and assignments will take place at the various portfolio checkpoints or intervals that are built into the timelines. Feedback from reviewers during these earlier portfolio checkpoints is to be included in the portfolio as evaluative reflections, serving to support the holistic scoring process (see Chapters 2 and 3).

Because the portfolio is designed to be scored, it may become part of the program's or college's overall assessment and accountability system. Many universities are moving in this direction as commercial electronic portfolio programs, such as TaskStream and FolioLive, offer strong management tools to assist in scoring and documentation. More will be said

of these programs and electronic portfolios in Chapter 7. PATT (2000) emphasizes that scoring portfolios can appear challenging due to their "open ended" nature, which can yield a range of responses. For this reason, it is imperative to have professional development for all scorers and evaluators in scoring the portfolio, along with collaboration and agreement on the criteria, standards, and rubrics or scoring guides. Program faculty and administrators should also collectively practice scoring the same portfolio samples in order to build consistency and reliability into the scoring process. Candidates could also do mock scoring of assignments and "working portfolios" as part of their course activities. These types of scoring activities are built into the portfolio timelines and checkpoints described in Tables 4.5 and 4.6. Scoring activities such as these further allow program instructors and candidates to internalize the program standards and portfolio rubrics. They also allow for the portfolio scoring process to be broken down into predictable and manageable intervals to be shared by candidates as well as instructors.

General Portfolio Scoring Procedure

A general portfolio scoring procedure is one strategy recommended by PATT (2000) designed to provide a simple feel for the portfolio and to minimize the time it takes to score. It involves three main steps:

- *Start with a brief scan of the entire portfolio to get a general sense of its contents, organization, and purpose.* There is no detailed reading by the scorer at this point, only general impressions.

- *Read the Portfolio Executive Summary, and review the artifact selected by the candidate as the best evidence of the standard or parameter under consideration.* Compare the item to the rubric or anchor piece to decide on a score. This should be done quickly to get a general view of the candidate's level of proficiency. It is important that candidates are given clear directions on writing portfolio summaries and reflections, because they serve as critical guides to scorers and reviewers of the portfolio and the relevance of each artifact for demonstrating competence of a specific standard. Please see Chapter 3 for suggestions on writing portfolio reflections. Chapters 5 and 6 give additional suggestions on organizing and presenting the portfolio so that it is most effective in presenting the candidate's proficiencies.

- *Skim the remainder of the portfolio for further evidence beyond the initial score.* The scorer reviews other artifacts to support the standard and to guide in determining the actual level of proficiency, fluctuating between the higher or lower score.

The holistic scoring procedure is based on a process of estimating the proper score on the rubric. As an example, in the three-point portfolio rubric sample provided in Table 4.11, the line between *Credit* and *No Credit* is essentially the dividing line between proficient work and work that is not proficient. After looking at the primary evidence for the standard or parameter, the scorer should try to form an impression of whether or not the candidate demonstrates proficiency. This means that the scorer will always start on the *Credit/No Credit* line and initially fall onto the "proficient" side or the "not proficient" side. Once the scorer gets on the side of proficiency, the rest of the artifacts in the portfolio are considered to decide which of the two levels of proficiency is appropriate. For instance, if the scorer decides initially that the work seems proficient in the parameter for *Content Knowledge in Planning and Instruction,* he or she would then be deciding only between levels *Credit* and *Exceeds Standard.* If the work is not proficient, then the decision would be *No Credit.* This appears to be an easier approach for some people to use.

Once a given portfolio has received scores in all standards or parameters, the program instructors will need to decide if, and, or how the collective scores will be converted into a letter grade, a percentage score, points, and so forth, and how much influence this will carry in determining a candidate's

Table 4.11 Sample Rubric for Teaching Credential Candidates

Directed Teaching/Demonstration of Competencies Evaluation Rubric

INTASC Principle 1	*Knowledge of Subject Matter*	
No Credit	Credit	Exceeds Standard
Candidate provides little or no evidence of subject-matter mastery, understanding of available classroom materials, and capacity to integrate appropriate subject matter into lesson plans.	Candidate provides sufficient evidence of subject-matter mastery, understanding of available classroom materials, and capacity to integrate appropriate subject matter into lesson plans.	Candidate provides consistent and ample evidence of subject-matter mastery, ability to adapt and augment available classroom materials to meet student needs, and capacity to integrate appropriate subject matter into lesson plans based on student progress and interests.
INTASC Principle 5	*Classroom Motivation and Management*	
No Credit	Credit	Exceeds Standard
Candidate is unable to use instructional time effectively or efficiently. Candidate provides little or no evidence of the ability to develop and maintain expectations of appropriate student behavior. Candidate does not develop a productive learning climate or consider alternative classroom management routines to build one.	Candidate uses instructional time effectively and efficiently. Candidate provides evidence of the ability to create and maintain an environment for effective student learning along with expectations of appropriate student behavior. When classroom problems arise, candidate seeks solutions through alternative classroom management routines.	Candidate provides clear, consistent, and convincing evidence for the effective and efficient use of instructional time. Candidate consistently provides evidence of the ability to create and maintain an effective environment for student learning along with clear and consistent expectations of appropriate student behavior. When classrooms problems arise, candidate anticipates solutions by implementing alternative classroom management routines.

INTASC Principle 7	*Instructional Planning*	
No Credit	Credit	Exceeds Standard
Candidate provides little or no evidence of planning for instruction. Plans do not reveal knowledge of state standards; integrate appropriate content; describe and align goals, materials, strategies, or assessment methods; use whole class and small groups; and connect to prior and future instruction.	Candidate provides sufficient evidence in planning for short-and long-range instruction. Plans show knowledge of state standards; describe and align goals, materials, strategies, and assessment methods; integrate appropriate content; use whole class and small groups; integrate available instructional technology; connect to prior and future instruction; and connect with students' lives, interests, and instructional needs.	Candidate provides consistent and ample evidence in planning for short- and long-range instruction. Plans show knowledge of state standards; describe and align goals, varied materials, strategies, and multiple assessment methods; integrate appropriate content; use whole class and small groups; employ effective technology; and clearly connect to prior and future instruction, students' cultures and interests, instructional needs, and other disciplines.

SOURCE: Adapted from CSULA CCOE Single Subject Credential Rubric, January 15, 2004. Reprinted by permission.

overall score. This decision will vary from instructor to instructor and from program to program. Because converting the level of proficiency from a rubric to a comprehensive score or letter grade can be problematic, a formula should be discussed and agreed on in advance for how the conversion will be made. Other scoring rubrics for portfolio presentations and portfolio documents are found in Chapter 6 and on the CD.

Recommendations for the Holistic Scoring of Portfolios

In dealing with a large number of portfolios (or any work), people become more reliable when they become more efficient. Therefore, speed and efficiency are important in getting through the workload. The following recommendations are offered:

- Concentrate on one parameter at a time.
- Do a 35-second scan of the entire portfolio.
- Read the Portfolio Summary and look where the *candidate* has directed you (also decide on what you believe is an appropriate score).
- Read the remaining work. Use the supporting evidence to complete scoring.
- Do not attempt to "read into the work." Score based only on the evidence presented.
- Score the parameters based on the rubrics in the scoring guide.
- Do proceed efficiently.
- Value the correct and insightful work and encourage the candidate to strive for excellence, not perfection.
- Focus on whether or not the work fulfills portfolio parameters rather than on the individual assignment requirements.
- The instructors should use the Portfolio Summary as a guide in scoring the portfolio.
- Pay attention to pictures, figures, tapes, and so forth, but do not be swayed by "glitz."

SOURCE: Adapted from PATT (2000).

Summary

The purpose of this chapter was to provide critical ideas and strategies for managing the portfolio implementation process. Throughout the chapter, both candidate assessment and evaluation, along with program assessment and evaluation, have been emphasized. Portfolios have been shown to be organized, goal-driven, living documents when implemented with careful planning and collaboration. Portfolios are also a valuable resource for providing concrete evidence that targeted program goals are being presented and mastered by the candidates. Still, just as it is necessary to identify specific criteria and parameters for assessing candidates, it is also necessary to identify specific criteria and parameters for assessing the effectiveness of programs, courses, or workshops. Through portfolio implementation, a continuous process is established for evaluating and improving programs based on concrete data resulting from the cyclical nature of portfolio development. Inherent in portfolio development are projection, planning, reflection, inquiry, and collaboration. These essential elements lead to the success of any program. When program parameters are clearly established and integrated into the portfolio process, along with establishing timelines and benchmarks, the portfolio process is more easily managed and the scoring of the portfolio is shared. This type of process helps in making the portfolio a transparent process whose value is understood by both candidates and instructors. In the next chapter, the contents of the portfolio are discussed more specifically.

Useful Resources

The following resources will be useful in developing your portfolio implementation plan.

INTASC (Interstate New Teacher Assessment and Support Consortium) Web site: http://www.ccsso.org/Projects/Interstate_New_Teacher_Assessment_and_Support_Consortium/

Online Professional Development from Johns Hopkins and Morgan State Universities on the Portfolio Development Process: http://www.sitesupport.org/module1/portfproc.htm

Pennsylvania Assessment Through Themes (PATT). (2000). *Portfolio Implementation Guide*. Retrieved August 25, 2005, from http://www.pde.state.pa.us/fam_consumer/lib/fam_consumer/20/23/portig.pdf

Practical Assessment, Research and Evaluation—A peer-reviewed electronic journal: http://PAREonline.net/getvn.asp?v=7&n=4

Rubrics for Web Lessons: http://edweb.sdsu.edu/webquest/rubrics/weblessons.htm

Samples of student reflections based on INTASC Principles: http://www.sitesupport.org/module1/INTASC_PRINCIPLE_1_1.htm

5

Contents of the Portfolio

The portfolio is most definitely an authentic assessment of candidates. The portfolio is not only a collection of the work completed, but it represents what we are capable of doing and what we have learned. The portfolio is, in a sense, a representation of us, the students, and the university as well as the professors who have influence us, the students. (Candidate Reflection)

Chapter Objectives

The reader will be able to

- develop a table of contents;
- develop an introduction and/or an executive summary;
- develop a vision and/or educational philosophy;
- identify and develop personal documents for inclusion, such as an updated resume;
- develop reflective introductions to professional standards;
- describe how to identify, select, and organize artifacts to demonstrate competency in professional standards;
- review the importance of summative reflections on the overall learning experience and quality of the program.

Scenario

José was in the last semester of his teaching credential program. Denise, a colleague of José, also was completing requirements for her teaching credential. The completion of a portfolio that demonstrated their competencies in the standards designated by the state was a major requirement.

One day after a faculty meeting at their school, José and Denise were walking to their cars to attend their university class. José mentioned that he had been gathering a lot of stuff for the portfolio, but he was not sure whether he had the right documents or if he was missing information. Denise expressed the same concerns. She commented, "I have loads of stuff! What do we need besides our evidence for each teaching standard? Someone told me that I needed a resume. Someone else said I needed a vision or a philosophy. I am getting worried. I hope the professor will tell us what to include." José expressed the same sentiment. He also mentioned that it might be useful if he could look at some sample successful portfolios that had been done by other students.

A similar conversation was taking place among a group of administrative credential candidates who also had to assemble portfolios. John was commenting on the portfolio process to fellow colleagues: "When I first heard of the portfolio, I thought, 'No problem!' I'm a teacher and I've used portfolios in my school with my elementary students. I know how helpful they are for showing growth in my elementary students and helping them to evaluate themselves. Still, I did not really understand what I was in for as an administrative credential candidate. Portfolios are a lot of work! The process really helped me to think about what I was doing in each class and why, and how that class or assignment would help me to grow as an administrator. The portfolio helped me to stay focused on the big picture of becoming a school principal. Having to keep and organize assignments into artifacts also helped me to think more deeply about each assignment and how it assisted me in developing skills and abilities as an administrator. I was constantly putting myself under a microscope to view and evaluate my progress. Completing an assignment was not enough until I figured out what that assignment or activity had to do with my overall profile as an administrator, or educational leader. When I developed a workshop for paraprofessionals on legal issues surrounding their roles and responsibilities, I saw how this one activity addressed several administrative standards. The portfolio process helped me to clearly identify each standard and to cross-reference assignments, artifacts, and activities when appropriate."

Overview

The aspiring teacher and administrator candidates in the scenario are viewing the portfolio process through different experiential lenses. John has had some experience. He has used portfolios with his students. However, he is now experiencing the process as an adult learner. John also appears to have some familiarity with how to develop the portfolio, whereas José and Denise seem uncertain about what is expected. Even though candidates may be aware that they have to develop a portfolio, they are often unsure of what the most appropriate contents for the portfolio are and how to select them. Nearly all are clear that they must collect evidence linked to standards. Therefore, coursework and field artifacts usually are accumulated. However, many programs require that candidates in credential programs include other documents, such as a vision, a philosophy, previous credentials, professionally related certificates, a resume, and letters of recommendation.

Chapter 4 discussed the organization of the portfolio development process. Chapter 2 described how to systematically, over time, select, evaluate, and modify contents for inclusion. In this chapter, examples of typical portfolio contents are discussed and highlighted. The chapter begins with the cover page and table of contents to give an overview of the contents. Next, the introduction and summary statements are described, as well as how to develop the vision and/or philosophy and other documents to be included, such as a resume. Then a major section of the portfolio, which contains artifacts that provide evidence of levels of mastery in the standards, is addressed. The introduction to the professional standards, and how to select and organize artifacts to demonstrate competencies, is described. Also included is a table that can assist candidates in categorizing and cross-referencing artifacts to demonstrate levels of competency in two or more standards.

It is not our goal to show examples of all the possible ways that one might select contents for a portfolio, but rather to offer readers an idea of how they might develop, organize, and choose contents for their personal portfolios. Portfolio developers will need to tailor these suggestions to their personal circumstances. Most of the sample contents shown are for summative evaluation portfolios, because those portfolios are the most comprehensive. To a lesser extent, some examples of contents used to satisfy the requirements of formative portfolios are provided.

Portfolio Cover Page/Title Page

The *cover page* of the portfolio may be designed in the same way as a major paper, project, or book. Some programs may call for candidates to create a background design with specific information on the cover, and other programs may have guidelines for a specific format. Sometimes a photo of the candidate might be included. Table 5.1 displays typical information that may be placed on the cover page. Other examples are on the CD.

Table 5.1 Cover Page/Title Page (Sample)

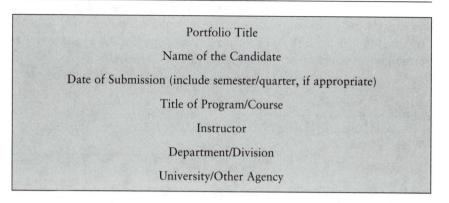

Portfolio Title
Name of the Candidate
Date of Submission (include semester/quarter, if appropriate)
Title of Program/Course
Instructor
Department/Division
University/Other Agency

Table of Contents

A well-organized portfolio will provide a table of contents. The *table of contents* gives an overview of the contents and their location in the portfolio. A table of contents that is skillfully organized can facilitate a coherent presentation of the evidence contained in the portfolio. It allows the reader or presenter to locate specific artifacts quickly.

Tables 5.2A, 5.2B, 5.2C, and 5.2D are sample tables of contents for an aspiring elementary teacher, a secondary teacher, an administrator, and a school counselor, respectively. The contents are organized generally by major subheadings: *Introduction* and/or *Executive Summary, Personal Information, Professional Standards* and a listing of artifacts linked to the standards, and *Reflections*. Examples of standards include the following: For teaching, the Interstate New Teacher Assessment and Support Consortium (INTASC) Standards. For leadership, the Interstate School Leaders Licensure Consortium (ISLLC): Standards for School Leaders Standards. For counseling, examples of activities are presented that counselors may be expected to engage in that are related to the National Standards for School Counseling Programs (NSCP). The standards are included on the CD. Programs and candidates most likely will need to tailor their portfolio artifacts to regional or state standards. The examples show how a table of contents might look for hard-copy portfolios. Note that Tables 5.2B and 5.2C (Sample Portfolio Table of Contents for Teacher Candidates, and Sample Portfolio Table of Contents for Administrator Candidates) show how artifacts may be used to demonstrate accomplishments in more than one standard. Table of contents designs for electronic portfolios are displayed in Chapter 7 but follow the same basic guidelines presented here. The primary differences are the options

for organizing the table of contents based on technology, such as hyperlinks and software programs. Each major section and subsection of the table of contents should be arranged in a binder or similar container with section dividers, tabs, and/or other organizing features, which will expedite quick location of contents. Sample tables are included in the CD.

Table 5.2 Sections for the Portfolio Contents

Section	*Contents*
Introduction	Overview/executive summary of the portfolio
Personal and Background Information	Personal statement Vision Philosophy Resume Letters of reference Credentials and certificates Transcript from colleges, universities
Professional Competencies	Professional standards with documentation (artifacts) of competencies
Reflections of the Course/Program	Include reflections that are formative and summative. There may be reflections in the section on standards

Table 5.2A Sample Elementary Teacher Candidate Portfolio Table of Contents

(Examples of Three Standards)	
Table of Contents Introduction	**Yellow Tab**
Personal Information • Philosophy of Education • Philosophy of Classroom Management • Diversity Statement • Resume • Application to XYZ School District • Transcripts • Exams • References/Letters of Recommendation	**Orange Tab**

Field Work and Directed Teaching (Including Learner's Products)	**Clear Tab**
Principle 3 (Adapting Instruction to Individual Needs) • Weekly Objectives/Lesson Plans • Suggestions for Modifying Lessons and Room Arrangement for Students (classroom maps) • Specific Examples of Different Types of Modifications (ELL, Inclusion)	**Red Tab**
Principle 8 (Assessment of Student Learning) • Language and Literacy Assessment Reading Case Study Alternate Ranking-Reading High-Frequency Spanish Word List Spanish Running Record and Comprehension Questions Spanish Reading Inventory Record • General Content Area Assessment Second-Grade Content Standards—Science Center Third-Grade Content Standards—Thematic Unit • Scoring Guides Writing Rubric Math Rubric	**Blue Tab**
Principle 9 (Professional Commitment and Responsibility) • Back-to-School Night Information Documents and Video • Critiques From Mentor • Principal Observations and Evaluation • Parent Links/Communications Welcome/Homework Letter Parent Call Log • Workshops/Professional Development • Conference Presentations • Professional Memberships • Service Learning/Community Service	**Purple Tab**
Reflections • Growth Reflections • Program Reflection • Reflections of the Portfolio Process	**Green Tab**

Table 5.2B Sample Secondary Teacher Candidate Portfolio Table of Contents

Single Subjects (Secondary)	
Contents	*Section*
Personal Information Philosophy of Education Diversity Statement Autobiography Curriculum Vitae References/Letters of Recommendation Transcripts	I
Teaching Standards (Example of Four Standards) **Principle 1: Knowledge of Subject Matter** Written Lesson Plans (Five Best Examples) Course Final Research Paper: *Strategies for Promoting Literacy With Culturally Diverse Populations* Fieldwork and Directed Teaching Logs and Student Work **Principle 2: Knowledge of Human Learning and Development** Assessment Records and Plans for Improvement of Learning Student Reflection on Learning With Collaborative Groups Recordkeeping Logs Fieldwork and Directed Teaching Logs and Student Work **Principle 4: Multiple Instructional Strategies** Video of Student and Teacher Engagement During Instruction Written Lesson Plans (Five Best Examples) Course Final Research Paper: *Strategies for Promoting Literacy With Culturally Diverse Populations* Fieldwork and Directed Teaching Logs and Student Work **Principle 5: Classroom Motivation and Management** Classroom Management Plan Video of Student and Teacher Engagement Fieldwork and Directed Teaching Logs and Student Work	II
Reflections	III
Exams	IV

Table 5.2C Sample Administrator Candidate Portfolio Table of Contents

Contents	*Description*	*Artifacts/Evidence*
Executive Summary	Overview of the Portfolio	Executive Summary
Philosophy of Education	Program Philosophy	Initial and End-of-Program Philosophy
	Example of Three Standards	
Standard 1 **(Facilitating the Vision)**	A school administrator is an educational leader who promotes the success of all students by facilitating the development, articulation, implementation, and stewardship of a vision of learning that is shared and supported by the school community.	1. Vision 2. Single School Plan for Student Achievement–Description and Intent 3. Memorandums About Meetings for Social Studies Department Vision Development 4. Single School Plan for Student Achievement (Division of Work) 5. Examples of Agendas and Minutes for Social Studies Department Meeting 6. Teacher Evaluations of Meetings 7. Example of Agenda for First Critical Friends Meeting 8. Memorandum About Vision Comments by Social Studies Department

(Continued)

Table 5.2C (Continued)

Contents	*Description*	*Artifacts/Evidence*
Standard 2 (**School Culture and the Instructional Program**)	A school administrator is an educational leader who promotes the success of all students by advocating, nurturing, and sustaining a school culture and instructional program conducive to student learning and staff professional growth.	1. Professional Development PowerPoint 2. Equity Report on Test Scores in U.S. History, Regular and Gifted Classes, at Sunshine Middle School 3. Equity Report on Tracking at Sunshine Middle School 4. Critical Analysis of Special Education in Sunshine Middle School 5. Critique on Instructional Program 6. Transformation Plan for Sunshine Middle School
Standard 3 (**Managing the Organization**)	A school administrator is an educational leader who promotes the success of all students by ensuring management of the organization, operations, and resources for a safe, efficient, and effective learning environment.	1. Case Study on Sunshine Middle School 2. Equity Report on Tracking at Sunshine Middle School 3. Transformation Plan for Sunshine Middle School 4. Teacher's Handbook 5. Redesigned Social Studies Department Curriculum 6. Professional Development Documents on Standards Implementation

Table 5.2D Sample School Counselor Portfolio Table of Contents

	Statement of Purpose
Section 1	**Personal Background**
1.1	Worldview
1.2	Professional Experiences Related to Counseling
1.3	Academic Background and Current Coursework
1.4	Professional Association Membership
1.5	Honors, Awards, Grants
1.6	Publications
1.7	Certificates, Credentials, and Licenses (Title and Number)
1.8	Letters of Recommendation and Commendation
1.9	Specialized Skills
1.10	Current Resume
1.11	Community Involvement/Volunteer Service
1.12	Mentor/I Experiences
1.13	Political, Legislative Advocacy
Section 2	**Standard A: Academic**
2.1	Comprehensive Guidance Program
2.2	Plan for Student Results
2.3	Results Data
2.4	Reflections and Analysis of Data
2.5	Other Contributions
2.6	Personal Reflections
Section 3	**Standard B: Career**
3.1	Guidance Curriculum Units
3.2	Guidance/Career Center Plan
3.3	Classroom Visitations
3.4	Student Personal Statements
3.5	Videos of Career Activities
3.6	Photographs of Career Libraries
3.7	Readings
3.8	Technology Applications
3.9	Journal, Learning Logs
3.10	Personal Reflection and Critique
Section 4	**Standard C: Personal Social Development**
4.1	Guidance Curriculum Units
4.2	Guidance/Career Center Plan
4.3	Presentations
4.4	Videos of Student Activities
4.5	Written Contributions (Newsletters, Articles, Publications)

Introduction and/or Executive Summary for the Portfolio

The *introduction* or *executive summary* gives an overview of the purpose and major features of the portfolio. The introduction should set the tone in ways that engage the reader to anticipate a quality product that is reflective and one that provides substantive evidence of the candidate's performance in the required competencies. Table 5.3 presents an example of a portfolio introduction.

Table 5.3 Sample Introduction to the Portfolio

Introduction

The contents of this portfolio cover the last two years of my work at Sunshine State University, as well as many activities that I did at Central High School as an English teacher in a large comprehensive high school. I am presenting a range of documentation that demonstrates my understanding and competency in the principles. Many of these documents show my knowledge, skills, and dispositions for equity and my ability to work as a teacher in a culturally and linguistically diverse school.

I want to especially thank the many instructors and supervising teachers who have contributed to my growth in so many ways. They have given their time and expertise to provide support and guidance in the development of my vision and educational philosophy. Through our collective efforts, I have learned to look at the data of our school and see the inequities that we face daily. My work of the last two years has led me to look deeper at the meaning of what quality classes and schools should be like, to grow as a teacher, to gain skills in instructing students to attain a goal, and to understand the fundamental issues and strategies that are needed to be an effective teacher in an urban school.

Over the last two years, I have been working collaboratively with students, parents, administrators, staff, professors, and fellow candidates in my teacher credential program. I did individual projects and often worked collaboratively with a variety of individuals. Much of the work was done beyond the normal school day, often on weekends and late into the evening. The work in this portfolio demonstrates my completion of the goals and standards set by the School of Education at Sunshine University and by the state.

This is a living document and will go through many revisions as I continue to grow as a teaching professional. I plan to use this portfolio as an ongoing reflective document. I will add, delete, and revise its contents. I also plan to use it for future interviews.

Vision and Philosophy

Most programs require that candidates write a well-crafted vision that is developed over time. Research has established a relationship between vision and school effectiveness (Barth, 1990).

The development of a *vision* should be considered an important undertaking. It may be a short or a long discussion of what candidates view as their desired educational future. It may include what they expect to accomplish for students and themselves, and/or how they expect to influence the setting in which they work. It should address their personal knowledge, skills, and dispositions. The vision usually reflects the personal beliefs and values of the writer. Barth (1990) gives some useful ways to think about and write one's vision. He states that visions can emerge from such questions as, "When I leave this school I would like to be remembered for . . ."; The kind of school I would like my children to attend would . . ."; or "The kind of school I would like to teach in . . ." (p. 148). He describes a personal vision as "one's overall conception of what the educator wants the organization to stand for; what its primary mission is; what its basic, core values are; a sense of how all the parts fit together; and, above all, how the vision maker fits into the grand plan" (p. 148).

Table 5.4 Sample Teaching Vision

My Vision for Teaching

Becoming a teacher has been a lifelong dream. I have always wanted to be a positive influence in the lives of young people. When I was in grade school, my friend and I played school. I was always the teacher.

The teacher preparation program has helped me to gain a better understanding about the teaching profession. As a result of this program, I believe that I have the knowledge, skills, and disposition to become an outstanding teacher. I have begun to develop a vision of what I would like to happen for children in my classroom. I know that I will constantly revise this vision over the course of my career.

I desire to teach in a school where there is a diverse population. I want to be the kind of teacher who cares about who my children are and one who is able to communicate a caring feeling to my students and their parents. I want all of my students to believe that they are able to achieve high academic standards and that they can be successful in their future schooling and careers. My students will love to come to school and will have respect for adults and their classmates. I want my students to be confident and have the skills to succeed. When students leave my

Table 5.4 (Continued)

classroom, I envision that I will stay in contact with them and that their experiences in my classroom will have a long-term, positive effect. I expect to hear that my students are doing well in the upper grades.

I know that some aspiring teachers do not have the same beliefs and expectations for all kids as I do. It is my vision that as I gain more knowledge, confidence, and success as a teacher, I would like to help my peers see the great potential of all children.

I have a passion for teaching and am excited about being able to fulfill my lifelong dream!

The *philosophy* statement presents the candidate's viewpoint about the educational enterprise. Like the vision, the philosophy usually reflects the candidate's attitude, beliefs, and values about education. During the course of a program, a candidate will formulate and revise his or her philosophy, one that hopefully reflects growth and development. A sample philosophy is in Table 5.5.

Candidate Documents

Many programs view the portfolio as an ongoing *professional document* that offers the potential for continuous retooling or revision. Candidates are often encouraged or required to include documents that enhance their portfolios beyond solely providing evidence of meeting competency standards. Many candidates are using their portfolios in preparation for job interviews and also are bringing them for presentations during interviews. This is discussed further in Chapter 8.

Some of these documents are an *updated resume, credentials, certificates, college/university transcripts,* and *letters of recommendation.* Candidates should take time prior to including these documents to obtain reviews from experienced and knowledgeable professionals. Instructors and site supervisors can provide suggestions for resume development and recommend how to secure letters of recommendation. In consultation with instructors, candidates may want to include other relevant documents that reflect their unique skills and talents.

We have provided some sample links that include resume formats on the CD with related Web links. It is also useful for candidates to visit their

Table 5.5 Sample Philosophy

Philosophy

Sunshine State University

Name: Future Teacher

Date:

PHILOSOPHY OF EDUCATION STATEMENT

(Sample)

I believe that one major factor in improving K–12 schools rests on valuing each and every child regardless of his or her individual background and circumstances. Educators must strive to be responsive to every child and have an understanding of the knowledge, skills, and dispositions that they will need to be successful with their students. Great effort must be made to consider the factors that encompass each individual. I realize that this is a challenging goal, especially when there are so many students in a classroom; however, every interaction with a child must make a positive impact.

Another factor that needs to be addressed is improving parent involvement and school relations. If this is done effectively, I believe it would greatly improve student outcomes. Establishing a good relationship between teachers and parents should result in a greater understanding of how the child learns and how the learning can continue at home. Agreement among teachers and parents in learning and in discipline techniques is especially beneficial to students.

Improving the reading and writing skills of all children is essential. Students must be encouraged and supported to read and write in ways that result not only in academic competency but also in enjoyment of learning. Literacy development must be integrated with oral language to encourage students to be creative. Creativity leads to a revelation about the many possible ways one can express one's learning.

Educators must constantly be engaged in improving professional sources for learning and classroom working conditions if they are to be effective in teaching. I believe that teachers need to be patient and caring with all of their students. Classroom climates must be trusting and nurturing so students feel safe and secure. If a safe, secure climate exists, children will feel free to take risks and to ask questions. They will be more likely to explore, to be creative, and to be unafraid of failure. These are the kinds of classrooms that unlock the genius in children. This is what I hope for my children and my school.

university career centers and human resources departments at their workplace to obtain information on resume development.

Some of the features your resume should include are the following:

1. Name, address, work, home, and cell phone numbers; e-mail address
2. Career objective (e.g., teaching, school administrator, school counselor, curriculum specialist)
3. Personal qualifications (e.g., education, additional professional development, workshops)
4. Employment history (most recent first)
5. Publications
6. Presentations
7. Specialized skills (highlight those that are relevant to the position you are seeking—e.g., bilingual, certification in visual impairment, mentor teacher)
8. Any accomplishments, honors, awards, or grants (e.g., dean's list, honor societies, National Science Foundation [NSF] Science Through Literacy Grant, Bilingual Teaching Fellow)
9. References/letters of recommendation (professional references are preferred, such as employers/supervisors in related fields, former or current instructors, mentors)

Standards and Artifacts

If the portfolio is organized to demonstrate accomplishments in meeting standards, a *reflective introduction* to each standard is recommended. There was a full discussion about reflective statements in Chapter 3, and we suggest a review of that chapter. The introduction should reflect on the candidate's development and growth related to the standard. We urge that candidates provide a rationale describing why each artifact presents solid evidence of competency in the standard or a particular aspect of the standard. Tables 5.6A and 5.6B show examples of an introductory reflection to a standard for teacher and administrator candidates.

Portfolio artifacts provide tangible evidence to show a candidate's level of mastery/competency in a professional standard. Care must be taken in selecting artifacts. Selected artifacts should be those that best demonstrate competencies. Chapter 2 provides a comprehensive process of ways to transform artifacts into evidence. Artifacts may represent current levels of mastery in

Table 5.6A Sample Introduction to a Standard for a Teacher Credential Candidate

Interstate New Teacher Assessment and Support Consortium (INTASC)

Principle 1

Knowledge of Subject Matter

The teacher understands the central concepts, tools of inquiry, and structures of the discipline(s) he or she teaches and can create learning experiences that make these aspects of subject matter meaningful for students.

One of the first and most basic requirements of teachers is to know the subjects they teach. Knowledge of subject matter involves much more than simple facts or information about a specific content area, such as language arts, mathematics, social studies, science, art, music, or physical education. It also involves a strong understanding of the curriculum resources, instructional strategies, and classroom organizational structures to bring life to each content area. It further requires a clear understanding of the national, state, and district standards for each subject, along with the frameworks or curricular guidelines of what material to cover at each level. These are usually presented in the scope and sequence overviews for each subject and grade level.

Artifacts

In the Teacher Credential program we were given numerous activities and assignments to familiarize us with the various content areas, such as where and how to locate content standards and curriculum frameworks so that we could align our lessons to the appropriate standards. I have included several standards-based lesson plans, which I developed and implemented during my internship. We were also required to conduct *field observations* in classrooms where the subjects were being taught, along with reviewing and evaluating curriculum resources to enhance understanding and teaching to a wide range of students.

I've included two of my *midterm exams*, in which we were asked to prescribe types of programs and materials that would be appropriate for teaching mathematics or science to English-language learners along with a theoretical foundation to support our recommendations. We were also asked to develop thematic units around several content areas that made practical, real-world connections for the student. I've included an *inquiry-based thematic social studies unit* on elections and the primary role they play in our government. This unit included field trips, learning centers, group projects, applications of technology, letters to parents, and samples of completed student assignments that were given as assessment, in accordance with the curriculum framework for social studies in the fifth grade.

Lastly, I've included my passing RICA (Reading Instruction Competency Assessment) Examination and Praxis II Subject Assessments (Professional Assessments for Beginning Teachers) Scores as further evidence of subject matter mastery. I successfully passed both tests on my first attempt.

NOTE: RICA Examination and Praxis II Subject Assessments information available at http://www.rica.nesinc.com/ and http://www.ets.org/praxis, respectively.

Table 5.6B Sample Introduction to a Standard for an Administrator Candidate

Interstate School Leaders Licensure Consortium (ISLLC): Standards for School Leaders

Standard 3

Managing the Organization

A school administrator is an educational leader who promotes the success of all students by ensuring management of the organization, operations, and resources for a safe, efficient, and effective learning environment.

Being an administrator is a very difficult task. There are many behind-the-scenes activities that go on during the day, and one needs to be aware of everything for the school to function well. Although very chaotic at times, the routine activities are the same every day: The school opens at 7:00 a.m., the children eat breakfast, they line up, and the teachers pick up their classes and teach. Although the leader of the organization has to be aware of the daily routines and what needs to happen for the school to function, he or she also has to be diligent in making sure that all the adults in the school are working in ways that ensure that the educational needs of the students are being met.

Artifacts

The leadership program prepared us to meet this standard by requiring us to take a look at the school that we work with and to write a *case study of our school* in order to learn important information about the school. This offered me the opportunity to develop my **knowledge** and **skills** in finding, collecting, and analyzing data about my school. I learned about a variety of achievement data and where to find it. I also learned how to look at and gain an understanding of the culture of my school and the implications for leading change.

After analyzing the school case study, we were asked to create a plan to transform the school to make it a better learning environment. This required us to work in collegial learning groups to accomplish a common goal and to pool our **knowledge and experiences.** These artifacts provide complex information about how to manage change through gaining the **knowledge and insights** to understand organizational cultures, cultural contexts of organizations, and building teams for transformation to accomplish short- and long-term goals. We had to work together and collaborate on the plan.

I have also included a copy of my *fieldwork log*. During my fieldwork experience, I had the opportunity to act as the administrator designee for several days. It was then that I truly got a feel of what running a school is like. During one of my fieldwork days, I had to make sure that the school was up and running by the time the children arrived at the door. There were substitutes that needed to be called, classrooms to be covered for late-arriving teachers, even times I had to call the legal office for advice. I have included a memo from my mentor that documents my successful accomplishments of these tasks. She also included comments about this in my evaluation, which is included as an artifact. These artifacts also document **skills and dispositions related to ISLLC Standard 3.**

The experience of being in charge of the school was intimidating; however, with the help of the people around me, I managed to get everything in order by the time the children were in the classroom.

the standards along three dimensions: (1) *knowledge*—What have I learned by attendance in classes and workshops, and by reading relevant materials related to the standard? (2) *skills*—What evidence do I have that I can effectively apply the knowledge in the professional setting? (3) and *dispositions*—What artifacts provide evidence that I have the beliefs, values, commitment, and desire to meet this standard? These three dimensions reflect three domains of learning: (1) the cognitive domain of knowledge (Bloom, 1956), (2) the psychomotor domain of physical or manual skills and abilities (Simpson, 1972), and (3) the affective domain of attitudes, dispositions, and beliefs (Krathwohl, Bloom, & Bertram, 1973). Table 5.7 gives examples of the three domains, along with suggestions for artifacts and the specific competencies they demonstrate.

Some artifacts provide evidence of competencies in more than one standard, particularly in fieldwork assignments with job-related responsibilities, such as case studies and unit plans. They also demonstrate competencies in multiple domains. The case study is a comprehensive assignment and addresses several INTASC principles, such as Principle 3 (Adapting Instruction to Individual Needs) and Principle 8 (Assessment of Student Learning). It also appears across all three learning domains described in Table 5.7. Please see the CD for an example of a case study. For this reason, it is useful to ask these questions when selecting artifacts:

- What kinds of content knowledge and/or skills are demonstrated?
- Is the artifact related to the competency in which I need to demonstrate development?
- How does this demonstrate the process of learning?
- Is this (are these) the best artifact(s) to document my progress?
- What professional job-related skills are demonstrated?
- What beliefs, values, and expectations are evident in the artifact?

Table 5.8 separates artifacts from different sources into specific categories. This type of information is useful in deciding where to locate artifacts for the portfolio, as well as in cross-referencing artifacts that may appear in multiple locations.

Categorizing and Cross-Referencing Artifacts

Some type of graphic organizer or other tool should be used to help give an overview of how the collected artifacts are aligned to the standards. The Artifact Organizer (Table 5.9) illustrates a way to organize the artifacts for

(Continued on page 112)

Table 5.7 The Three Dimensions of Competence and Their Corresponding Learning Domains, With Sample Artifacts

Knowledge	*Skills*	*Dispositions*
Cognitive Learning Domain What I know or have learned by attendance in classes, workshops, and through course readings and related literature. Research and theoretical information or knowledge base	**Psychomotor Learning Domain** Specific abilities and skills I have where I can apply my knowledge in authentic professional settings	**Affective Learning Domain** Beliefs, attitudes, values, commitment, and desire I have to meet the standard
Sample Artifacts • Essays, written reports • Traditional exams • Certificate of completion • Literature reviews • Summaries or annotated reports • Research projects • Case studies • Attendance at professional development locales • Memberships in professional organizations and subscriptions to professional journals • Theoretical introductions to assignments (case studies, thematic units, classroom management plans) • Course grades	Sample Artifacts • Essays, written reports • Research projects Case studies Action research • Literature reviews • Learning centers • Planning and implementing workshops • Thematic units • Pictures of bulletin boards, learning centers • Lesson plans • Organizational charts • Drawing floor plans • Classroom management plans (authentic application of theories) • Examples of math and literacy assessments • Technology application in plans (multimedia presentations) • Videotapes • Samples of student work and completed projects • Observations by literacy and mathematics instructors	Sample Artifacts • Philosophy of education • Reflections on assignments • Journal entries • Supervisor observation reports • Self- and peer evaluations • Documents on communication and collaboration • Parent letters • Letters of commendation • End-of-course reflections • Summative reflections • Videotapes • Responses from students and parents • Student achievement • Evidence of expectations in assignments, rubrics, comments on students papers • Case-study reflections

Table 5.8 Suggested Artifacts

Personal	*Knowledge/Academic Documents*	*Fixed Assignments*	*Job-Related*
• Vision • Philosophy • Resume • References and other letters • Credentials • Transcripts • Letters and awards that are related to growth	• Coursework • Reflections • Case studies, action research, research papers, and reports • Summaries/reflections on books, articles read • Class presentation • Use of Web sites • Knowledge and competencies in teaching diverse population • Participation in conferences, in-service, workshops • Lesson study	• Journals • Learning logs • Fieldwork activities • Project • Reports • Evidence of teamwork • Videos • Budget activities • Community involvement projects	• Personal assessments • Lesson plans, unit plans • Student academic progress • Instructional assessments • Newsletters • Presentations to faculty, parents, community • Videos • Evidence of decision making, problem solving, use of data • Use of technology • Grant applications • Strategic planning documents

Table 5.9 Sample Artifacts Signoff and Ratings Organizer Using INTASC Standards

Candidate Name: Denise Brown

Rating Key: M–Minimally meets standard S–Satisfactorily meets standard E–Exceeds standard

Artifact	*Principle 1 (Knowledge of Subject Matter)*	*Principle 2 (Knowledge of Human Development and Learning)*	*Principle 3 (Adapting Instruction for Individual Learning)*	*Principle 4 (Multiple Instructional Strategies)*	*Principle 5 (Classroom Motivation and Management)*	*Principle 6 (Communication Skills)*	*Principle 7 (Instructional Planning Skills)*	*Principle 8 (Assessment of Student Learning)*	*Principle 9 (Professional Commitment and Responsibility)*	*Principle 10 (Partnerships)*
Case Studies										
Rating	**M**	**S**	**M**							
Instructor	**Mims**	**Doyle**	**Johnson**							
Date	**3/03**	**6/03**	**6/03**							
Field Notes										
Rating	**S**	**S**	**M**	**M**	**S**				**S**	
Instructor	**Smith**	**Salcido**	**Bush**	**Smith**	**Pulido**				**Mims**	
Date	**12/04**	**12/04**	**3/04**	**3/04**	**3/04**				**3/04**	
Lesson Plans										
Rating		**S**	**S**	**S**			**S**			
Instructor		**Doyle**	**Nichols**	**Salcido**			**Johnson**			
Date		**6/04**	**6/04**	**6/04**			**9/05**			

NOTE: Mims, Smith, Doyle, etc. represent professors who have rated the competency level and who have provided written documentation to the candidate.

Table 5.9 (Continued)

Artifact	*Principle 1 (Knowledge of Subject Matter)*	*Principle 2 (Knowledge of Human Development and Learning)*	*Principle 3 (Adapting Instruction for Individual Learning)*	*Principle 4 (Multiple Instructional Strategies)*	*Principle 5 (Classroom Motivation and Management)*	*Principle 6 (Communication Skills)*	*Principle 7 (Instructional Planning Skills)*	*Principle 8 (Assessment of Student Learning)*	*Principle 9 (Professional Commitment and Responsibility)*	*Principle 10 (Partnerships)*
Instructional Assessments										
Rating	**S**							**E**		
Instructor	**Bush**							**Bush**		
Date	**12/03**							**6/06**		
Teaching Video										
Rating	**E**	**E**	**S**	**S**	**S**	**S**	**S**	**E**		
Instructor	**Mims**	**Salcido**	**Nichols**	**Smith**	**Pulido**	**Doyle**	**Johnson**	**Bush**		
Date	**6/06**	**6/06**	**6/06**	**6/06**	**6/06**	**3/06**	**3/06**	**9/05**		

(Continued from page 107)

easy cross-referencing and to see quickly (1) if there is sufficient evidence for each standard and (2) which artifacts could serve as documentation for more than one standard. By using this organizer, candidates are able to assess where they have sufficient or insufficient numbers of quality artifacts. In addition, some candidates have expanded its use to record books and publications that they have read to assess whether there are voids in their literature or knowledge bases. The organizer helps to answer the question, Is there a Swiss cheese effect? (i.e., are there holes, where there is no evidence or minimal evidence?)

When including artifacts, candidates need to organize the table of contents and the portfolio sections in ways to cross-reference particular artifacts. This organizer would be used over the course of the program. Tables 4.5 and 4.6 in Chapter 4 outline benchmark activities in portfolio development that include checks for signoff on competencies. Candidates' papers, field logs, and other artifacts can be rated and signed off in a timely manner by instructors, supervisors, and mentors on whether the documentation *minimally meets standard, satisfactorily meets standard, or exceeds standard*. The candidate could then indicate on the organizer the rating, the person who rated the artifact, and the date. Those rating the documents would use agreed-on scoring rubrics for consistency in ratings, using guidelines similar to those described in Chapter 4.

Reflections and Reflective Statements

Continuous written reflections are an essential component of the portfolio process. These reflections record developmental and summative information about a candidate's growth. Chapter 3 highlighted the importance and the role of the reflective process in professional growth and provided some reflective prompts and sample reflections. A review of this information is useful to guide the writing of reflections for inclusion in the portfolio.

Portfolios many include several types of reflective statements. For example, *developmental* reflections might be for each section and subsection of the portfolio. These reflections are more specific to the task at hand. End-of-course or interim program reflections may also be included. The most comprehensive reflection, however, is *summative* and reflects on the growth and development over the course of the program. It may reflect on the program in general, the portfolio process, and other information considered important to the candidate, the program, or both. See the sample case study in the CD for examples of a variety of reflections.

Summary

This chapter discussed the major types of contents that are included in portfolios and provided some examples of portfolio contents. First, information and examples were shown of tables of contents and the development of a vision and/or educational philosophy. Next, documents for inclusion, such as a resume, transcripts, and letters of reference, were presented. The section on standards provided information on developing reflective introductions and how to identify, select, and organize artifacts to demonstrate competency in professional standards.

Suggested ways to think about and organize artifacts were discussed, and then a description of the introduction to the professional standards and an explanation of how to select and organize artifacts to demonstrate competencies were presented. For each standard, it was recommended that candidates provide a rationale to describe how each artifact presents evidence of competency in the standard or a particular aspect of the standard. The chapter concluded with a discussion of the different types of reflections that may be included in the portfolio.

Useful Resources

Samples of candidate reflections based on INTASC Principles: http://www.sitesupport.org/module1/INTASC_PRINCIPLE_1_1.htm

Visit university career-placement offices.

The following Web sites on resumes were retrieved from Google.com on July 18, 2005. There are thousands of sites to help with resume writing. Some sites have professionals who will work online with you.

http://www.e-resume.net

http://www.CollegeBoard.com (see *Resume Writing 101*)

http://www.Monster.com (see *Monster Sample Resumes*)

http://www.resumewriters.com

http://www.totalresume.com

http://www.killer-resume-generator.com

http://www.resumefast.net

http://resume.info

For Further Reading

Barnes, P., Clark, P., & Thull, B. (2005). Web-based digital portfolios and counselor supervision. *Journal of Technology in Counseling, 3*(1). Retrieved May 2, 2005, from http://jtc.colstate.edu/Vo3-1/Barnes/Barnes.htm

Barth, R. S. (1990). *Improving schools from within: Teachers, parents, and principals can make the difference.* San Francisco: Jossey-Bass. Chapters 11 and 12 are very useful for vision development.

Boes, S. F., VanZile-Tamsen, C., & Jackson, C. M. (2001). Portfolio development for the 21st century school counselor. *Professional School Counseling, 4*(3), 229–231.

Campbell, C. A., & Dahir, C. A. (1997). *The national standards for school counseling programs.* Alexandria, VA: American School Counselor Association.

6

Presenting and Sharing the Portfolio

You do not have to have a perfect portfolio that you would show from cover to cover. What you do want to have is a collection of items that you can strategically draw on to support claims you wish to make about yourself.

—Satterthwaite and D'Orsi (2003, p. 148), *The Career Portfolio Workbook*

Chapter Objectives

Readers will be able to

- describe how to prepare and retool a portfolio for a presentation;
- develop presentation strategies;
- design ways to schedule, organize, and score portfolio presentations.

Scenario

There were three weeks before the end of the term, and the candidates in Instructor Brown's class were becoming anxious about their portfolio presentations. They had been told they would be given twenty to thirty minutes for presentations to an audience of colleagues, instructors, and school site supervisors. After the presentation, the audience would be given an opportunity to ask questions and make comments and recommendations.

The candidates had many questions, such as, What contents should we present? They had collected work representing two or more years of accomplishments. Should they present from each competency area? What artifacts should they present? What about their reflections, vision, resume, and other documents that they had included in the portfolio? Who was going to score their presentation and tell them whether they had passed?

Other concerns that came up about the presentations related to presenting a hard-copy versus an electronic portfolio. In this program, candidates had been given a choice of which format to use. Candidates who had chosen the electronic version wanted to know how they could share their portfolio. Would someone provide a projector? Should they bring their own computer? Those who had hard-copy portfolios were using binders and file boxes. They were concerned about how to handle and show their work.

These concerns made the instructor aware that the candidates needed more guidance in preparing for their portfolio presentations.

Overview

Presenting and sharing the portfolio provides another opportunity for a candidate to engage in reflections, to self-evaluate, to showcase accomplishments, and to demonstrate evidence of professional development. Portfolio presentations may be (1) a component for a candidate's course or program evaluation, (2) an enhancement for a job interview, or (3) an ongoing professional-development document that is used for both self- and supervisor evaluation. In any case, those who are creating a portfolio presentation need to develop skills in constructing a focused, compelling presentation that provides evidence of professional achievement in national, state, and/or local professional standards. Preparation for a presentation requires in-depth reflection (see Chapter 3) and organization of portfolio contents for ease of presentation to the target audience. Most candidates will benefit from some guidelines, opportunities to practice, critiques of their presentation, and suggestions on how they can self-evaluate their presentations prior to the scheduled presentation time.

The purpose and objectives need to determine the timing, setting, configuration (room arrangement), and style (informal versus formal) of the presentation. Presentations are also guided by whether the presentation is for a preservice program credential and/or graduation, a job interview, or professional development. Another factor that influences the presentation style is whether the portfolio is formative or summative. (See Chapter 2.) This chapter mainly describes summative presentations, but many of the suggestions can be used for formative presentations, as well. Many possibilities exist for presenting the portfolio, and this chapter offers a few suggestions that we hope will assist programs and candidates with the process. Future uses of the portfolio for academic and career advancement, along with additional ways to tailor the portfolio for these purposes, will be presented in Chapter 8. The remainder of this chapter is about preparing, organizing, presenting, and evaluating the portfolio presentation.

Tips for Preparing Your Presentation

Regardless of the format or venue (setting or location), some key questions should be asked and answered regarding the portfolio presentation. These are presented in Table 6.1. These questions address the general *who, what, why, when, where,* and *how* of the presentation

Table 6.2 summarizes other important information that should be considered in preparing for the presentation. This becomes a quick reference or a Portfolio Presentation Planner.

By combining Tables 6.1 and 6.2, a *Portfolio Presentation Planning Worksheet* is developed; this worksheet can be used to address the key questions and to form a type of template to guide the planning for the portfolio presentation in the critical areas that need to be addressed. The Portfolio Presentation Planning Worksheet, presented in Table 6.3, can also be used as an artifact after the presentation.

For a presentation, the well-developed portfolio needs only to be modified or adapted for a specific purpose. Only the best examples of high-quality evidence are presented, and those works should be keyed to the required national, state, or local professional standards. Selection of artifacts will require earnest reflection. At least two high-quality artifacts per professional standard should be considered. These artifacts demonstrate knowledge, skills, and/or dispositions related to the standard(s).

As noted in Chapter 5, some artifacts may address more than one standard. The Artifacts Organizer by INTASC (Interstate New Teacher Assessment and Support Consortium) Standards (Table 5.9), or other professional standards, can be of great assistance in helping to select artifacts. Those on which instructors, supervisors, and mentors have signed off and that *meet* or *exceed standards* should receive primary consideration for presentation. The rationales or reflections that were written to support the

Table 6.1 Key Questions for Preparing Portfolio Presentation

1. ***Who* Questions:**
   - Who is the audience?
   - Who will evaluate the presentation and/or portfolio?
   - Who will support and assist in preparing for the presentation?
2. ***What* Questions:**
   - What standards and/or goals am I addressing, and what artifacts need to be selected?
   - What is being assessed (e.g., personal information, standards, vision)?
   - What types of feedback will be provided?
   - What rubrics are being used to evaluate the presentation, and are they aligned to the purpose and goals?
   - What materials do I need for the presentation?
   - What is the appropriate attire?
3. ***Why* Questions:**
   - Why am I doing this presentation? (What are the purpose[s] and goals for the presentation?)
4. ***When* Questions:**
   - When will the presentation take place? (date and time)
   - When will I start to prepare my presentation?
   - When will I rehearse my presentation?
5. ***Where* Questions:**
   - Where will the presentation take place?
6. ***How* Questions:**
   - How will I use portfolio rubrics as guides in preparing both the portfolio and the presentation?
   - How much does the presentation count toward a grade, certification, graduation, securing a position, on-the-job evaluation, and so forth?
   - How much time will I have for the presentation?
   - How much time do I need to prepare for the presentation?

selection of particular artifacts are useful for scripting the presentation. (See Chapter 3 and Tables 5.6A and 5.6B.)

Organize the physical layout of the portfolio so information is easy to find, attractively presented, and easy for the audience to view. Highlight sections of the document that provide the best evidence of knowledge, skills, or dispositions related to the standards. Indicate whether you are highlighting knowledge, skills, or dispositions. The use of highlighters,

Table 6.2 Portfolio Presentation Planner

(Check or circle all that apply in each category)

Purpose	*Timing*	*Setting/ Location*	*Format/ Configuration*	*Style*	*Audience*	*Type*	*Materials*
Personal • Professional development • Reflection **Academic** • Formative program evaluation • Summative program evaluation **Professional** • Career advancement • Job interview **Other**	**Formative Evaluation** (During course or program as a checkpoint) **Summative Evaluation** (End of course or program)	Regular classroom Different classroom Office setting Conference room Home Job location	Whole class Large group (15–20+) Small group (3–5) Pair share (both partners share portfolios) Review panel Individual/ one-on-one Roundtable (everyone shares portfolio) Other	Formal presentation Informal discussion Question and answer Interview Dialogue Other	Peer(s) Supervisor(s) Mentor(s) Instructor(s) Potential employer(s) Program review panel Self Friend(s) Other	Hard-copy Electronic	Table Projector and screen Handouts/ summaries Portfolio-at-a-Glance (Campbell et al., 2004) Evaluation/ feedback forms Presentation rubrics Other

Table 6.3 Portfolio Presentation Planning Worksheet

Name: ______________________ **Date:** ______________

Key Questions (Provide answers for each)

- Are the purpose(s) and goals for the presentation clearly stated?
- What is being assessed (e.g., personal information, standards, vision)?
- What rubrics are being used to evaluate the presentation, and are they aligned to the purpose and goals?
- What types of feedback will be provided?
- Who will be the evaluator(s)?
- How much does the presentation count toward a grade, certification, graduation, securing a position, on-the-job evaluation, and so forth?
- How much time will I have for the presentation?
- When will the presentation take place, and how much time do I have to prepare?
- Where will the presentation take place, and what additional materials will I need, if any?
- Have I used the portfolio rubrics as guides in preparing both the portfolio and the presentation?

Portfolio Presentation Checklist (Check or circle all that apply in each category)

Purpose	*Timing*	*Setting/ Location*	*Format/ Configuration*	*Style*	*Audience*	*Type*	*Materials*
Personal • Professional development • Reflection **Academic** • Formative program evaluation	**Formative Evaluation** (During course or program as a checkpoint)	Regular classroom Different classroom Office setting	Whole class Large group (15–20+) Small group (3–5)	Formal presentation Informal discussion Question and answer	Peer(s) Supervisor(s) Mentor(s) Instructor(s) Potential employer(s)	Hard-copy Electronic	Table Projector and screen Handouts/ summaries

• Summative program evaluation **Professional** • Career advancement • Job interview **Other**	**Summative Evaluation** (End of course or program)	Conference room Home Job location	Pair share (both partners share portfolios) Review panel Individual/one-on-one Roundtable (everyone shares portfolio) Other	Interview Dialogue Other	Program review panel Self Friend(s) Other		Portfolio-at-a-Glance (Campbell et al., 2004) Evaluation/feedback forms Presentation rubrics Other

The Specifics of My Portfolio Presentation on [Date: _______________]

Who? (Audience) **What?** (Standards, etc.) **Why?** (Purpose) **When?** (Date/duration) **Where?** (Location/setting) **How?** (Configuration) **Materials** **Special Notes** **Reflections on Presentation**	

underlining, color coding, or bold or enhanced type is suggested. Some candidates use sticky notes with notations or tabs on the document to point out pertinent information. The CD provides some visual examples of presentation layouts.

The audience and the type of setting for the presentation should determine the most appropriate container for the presentation. Hard-copy materials may be housed in a binder, that is, a file that is transportable, expandable, and open at the top for easy access. Many office stores have milk-crate-type files that are open and lightweight. In programs in which portfolios have been developed over a several-year period, one may need to scale down and re-sort documents for presentation. A thumbnail summary of all documentation for each of the standards and levels of proficiency can be distributed in a table-of-contents format, table format, or modified Artifacts Organizer format. Campbell et al. (2001) describe a process called "Portfolio at a Glance" (p. 95), which highlights specific artifacts in ways that allows for a quick review of the portfolio. The process, which uses nine steps, is designed for teaching portfolios but could be adapted for administrator and counseling portfolios:

Writing the Brochure

1. *Reflect* on one standard at a time.
2. *Select* at least one artifact to feature within a standard.
3. *Focus* on the teaching behaviors that are evidenced in the one artifact.
4. *Reword* your teaching behaviors into concise, specific statements in the past tense.
5. *Clarify* your teaching behaviors by writing directly above the name of the artifact a short descriptor of the competency demonstrated.
6. *Continue* steps 1–5 for each standard.

Assembling the Brochure

7. *Cut and paste* the list of information using a larger piece of paper or a computer.
8. *Edit* the contents of your draft brochure.
9. *Select* desktop design software that will assemble your text to catch the reader's eye. (pp. 95–96)

All of these processes provide an overview of documentation that is linked to each of the standards. The materials in the binder or file folders can be encased with plastic inserts. Binders with pockets are useful for insertion of a floppy disk or a CD, which might contain media information for the presentation.

Electronic portfolios are becoming increasingly popular, and many programs are requiring electronic and Web folios. A Web address can be included on a resume. Chapter 7 of this book is devoted to discussing how to design, organize, and develop electronic portfolio using Word, PowerPoint, and Web-based formats. The benefits of electronic portfolios are highlighted in Chapter 7 along with information on how to prepare for electronic presentations. A crucial factor that needs to be addressed regarding electronic portfolios is the setting for presentation. It is essential that the proper lighting and equipment be available and tested prior to the presentation. Candidates should have a hard-copy backup in case of equipment failure.

Tips for Scheduling the Presentation

Plan the presentation for the required time block that is designed to meet the required goals and purposes (e.g., twenty- to thirty-minute time slots for each presentation). Timed presentations usually require rehearsing. If a high-stakes presentation is required, candidates might want to consider a rehearsal video that is staged for people who give useful critiques. Candidates might also want to use an audiotape. Further, the rubric in Table 6.2 helps candidates to critique rehearsal presentations. The CD presents examples of both hard-copy and electronic presentations.

Programs and instructors may use a variety of scheduling formats. In the end, each program has to review its purposes and standards for the presentation and then decide how the scheduling decisions might enhance or distract from the desired purposes and outcomes. When the contents of the portfolio previously have been rated for levels of proficiency in meeting standards, the presentation may be a culminating experience for candidates to share with one another their accomplishments. Another scenario might include instructors and field supervisors using the presentation as a component of a final evaluation on the demonstration of competencies. Yet another scenario might be giving candidates the opportunity to simulate a portfolio presentation for a job interview.

If portfolio presentations are designed to include a variety of audiences, it is essential to engage in long-range planning. Some programs, particularly certification- and degree-granting ones, might require candidates to present to supervisors, mentors, and/or colleagues in areas in which the candidates aspire or are currently working. When including audiences who work in different locations and settings and who may have competing calendars, one discovers that the logistics of scheduling are time-consuming. Prioritize who must attend the presentation, provide them with several alternative dates, and then determine optimal times for presentations. Supervisors and others will need to be granted adequate notice.

Prevent possible scheduling conflicts by scheduling some open time in the calendar for unexpected cancellations. It may be necessary for the candidate to do presentations at more than one location to accommodate school or district site field supervisors. If this format is used, quality assurance is needed. This should include, at a minimum, an orientation and professional development for all evaluators and a monitoring system for documenting and recording evaluations of the presentation and portfolio.

Supervisors, mentors, and others involved should be thoroughly informed about their roles related to the presentation and the scoring process. It is desirable for a candidate to schedule a meeting with evaluators in advance of the presentation. Some programs encourage candidates to leave their portfolios with their supervisor before or after the presentation. If the program implementation guidelines suggested in Chapter 4 are used, most supervisors and others who are involved in the candidates' development will be familiar with most aspects of their portfolios.

Candidates might want to reflect on what types of feedback they desire in addition to those required by their program. This will prove useful for their continued development. Candidates should follow up with letters of appreciation to anyone who assisted, supervised, or mentored them.

We suggest that candidates take time to think about appropriate attire for the presentation. Presentations should be treated as a professional experience in which candidates are given an opportunity to demonstrate achievement and receive feedback for further development. It also can be a time for experiencing what may take place in a job interview. It is important to consider the audience and setting for presentation in selecting attire. Professional attire is suggested for summative presentations and those that include professionals from the field in the audience.

Presentation Formats

There are a variety of presentation formats and schedules for portfolio presentations. Among the types of formats are

- presentations to a whole class or group of colleagues in one or two class sessions,
- end-of-course presentations during the program,
- presentations in small groups over several days,
- portfolio conferencing.

Presentation agendas are designed based on goals, purposes, and a time frame. Presenters need to check for understanding regarding expectations for the presentation, and then a presentation outline should be prepared. Table 6.4

Table 6.4 Sample Portfolio Presentation Outline

Name: **Portfolio:** **Date:**

Introduction and Vision	5–10 min.	**Purpose of Portfolio Presentation/Overview** • Give a personal introduction (e.g., name, current position, level in program) • Share personal vision, philosophy, and/or educational platform • State primary goals • Describe specific objectives Standard A Standard B Standard C
Standard A	5 min.	**Selected Artifacts and Key Points/Highlights** 1. Reflections on 1st artifact for Standard A 2. Reflections on 2nd artifact for Standard A
Standard B	5 min.	**Selected Artifacts and Key Points/Highlights** 1. Reflections on 1st artifact for Standard B 2. Reflections on 2nd artifact for Standard B
Standard C	5 min.	**Selected Artifacts and Key Points/Highlights** 1. Reflections on 1st artifact for Standard C 2. Reflections on 2nd artifact for Standard C
Discussion/ Question and Answer	10 min.	**Invite Dialogue and Conversation** **Respond to Audience Questions**
Adjournment		**Thank Audience** Determine how and when feedback will be provided (this may be done prior to presentation)

gives a sample *Portfolio Presentation Outline*. Please note that specific guidelines for the presentations vary. Guidelines for academic portfolio presentations should be provided in advance by the program or instructor. Candidates for preservice, graduation, credential, and program completion are usually familiar with what is expected.

A presentation may also include a brief summary of growth in the professional standards by having candidates share a table (i.e., Artifacts Organizer, *Portfolio at a Glance*) of their overall growth, reflections on the program, and the portfolio development experience.

Candidates should write letters or notes of appreciation to those who participated in the presentation.

When candidates are presenting in large-group settings, a rotation format may be used. In this setting, candidates are divided into groups of four to six and they present to colleagues while the instructor and/or mentors circulate from group to group. Guidelines and norms are provided and discussed on the agenda and how to conduct the presentations. The small-group setting allows candidates to take turns in presenting. Every candidate gets an opportunity to present. This gives all candidates an opportunity to showcase their work. This can be done in one or two class sessions. The peer group reviews and scores the presentation. Candidates might then leave their portfolios for instructors to evaluate. Other formats might include a group of candidates presenting over several days to their entire class. In this way, every candidate's presentation is heard by the entire group and the instructors hear every candidate's entire presentation. This setting presents a good opportunity for videotaping. Presenters would receive feedback from peers and instructors.

Table 6.5 shows a schedule that might be used for a summative presentation in a longer-term program in which the desired goal might be to have most or all of the instructors who have taught the candidates participate in a culminating activity. The format and schedule presented in Table 6.5 schedules five to six different candidates a day over several days. Each day a different group presents to an instructor who has taught in the program and to his or her peers. This enables all of the instructors to participate during one or more sessions and hear, firsthand, how candidates communicate their growth and development. Field site supervisors may also participate. This setting allows for meaningful exchange among colleagues and instructors, and for rich critiques of the information presented by the candidates. With this scheduling format, each candidate presents for twenty to thirty minutes and then receives feedback and scores for the presentation. After all candidates present, there can be time scheduled for comments, reflections, and so forth. Sample presentations of this small-group format are available on the CD.

Portfolio conferences provide another format for sharing the portfolio. Winsor and Ellefson (1998) have described the conferencing model as a valuable process for self-evaluation and collaborative evaluation. They emphasize the potential of the portfolio as a lifelong tool for reflection and evaluation, a topic discussed more fully in Chapter 8. This conferencing process can be used in addition to or possibly as an alternative to traditional portfolio presentations. Winsor and Ellefson portray the portfolio conference as an

Table 6.5 Sample Presentation Schedule: 200X Spring Quarter, Teacher Credential Portfolio Presentations

Professor Jones, School of Education, Sunshine University

May 28 Wednesday	May 29 Thursday	June 2 Monday	June 3 Tuesday
5:00–8:00 P.M. **5:00** Candidate A **5:40** Candidate B **6:20** Candidate C **7:00** Candidate D **7:40** Concluding comments/reflections *Professor A* *Field Supervisor B*	5:00–8:00 P.M. **5:00** Candidate E **5:40** Candidate F **6:20** Candidate G **7:00** Candidate H **7:40** Concluding comments/ reflections *Professor C* *Field Supervisor D*	6:30–9:20 P.M. **6:30** Candidate H **7:10** Candidate I **7:50** Candidate J **8:30** Candidate K **9:10** Concluding comments/ reflections *Professor B* *Field Supervisor A*	5:00–8:00 P.M. **5:00** Candidate L **5:40** Candidate M **6:20** Candidate N **7:00** Candidate O **7:40** Concluding comments/reflections *Professor D* *Field Supervisor C*
June 9 Monday 5:00–8:00 P.M. **5:00** Candidate P **5:40** Candidate Q **6:20** Candidate R **7:00** Candidate S **7:40** Concluding comments/reflections *Professor E* *Field Supervisor E*	June 10 Tuesday 5:00–9:20 P.M. Makeup day for candidates who need to reschedule presentations		

ongoing, dynamic formative model of assessment that engages the portfolio developer in the process of self-evaluation. Although they describe this process as mainly for student teachers, it has the potential to be adapted in a variety of settings and with other professionals, such as administrators and counselors.

The conferencing model uses student-led evaluation. In the conference, candidates share their perception of their development with supervisors. Supervisors then review *self-evaluations* and respond to the candidates. The responses of the supervisors are a significant component of the conferencing. Winsor and Ellefson recommend three guidelines for responding to student self-evaluations: "Responses should offer praise in respect to progress and achievement, offer expertise concerning any issues or questions raised by students' self-evaluation, and guide student teachers in setting goals for further development as professional educators" (p. 73).

Scoring the Presentation

Because many presentation possibilities exist, programs and instructors need to design rubrics and scoring procedures that are aligned with program and class standards using guidelines for rubric development. Candidates should receive scoring rubrics in advance of presentations to help them clarify expectations and terminology. This approach also gives candidates time to become familiar with the scoring indicators. Sometimes in using scoring rubrics, candidates may score *below standard* in one category but score *meets standard* or *exceeds standard* in another category. An overall score needs to consider all of the indicators, yet some indicators may have more importance than others. If so, indicators may be weighted in determining an overall score for the presentation.

Some questions that need to be asked when developing the rubric are:

1. What are the purposes for the presentation?
2. Who is (are) the audience(s)?
3. What content should be presented?
4. Is a specific communication style or format required?
5. What indicators should be used?
6. How will the presentation be weighted in the final class grade, certification, and/or program completion?
7. Who will score the presentation?

Videotapes of practice presentations can be used to establish agreed-on indicators for what a *below standard, meets standard,* or *exceeds standard* presentation looks like. Table 6.6A and Table 6.6B provide sample scoring rubrics. These are not for an evaluation of the portfolio but for how the information in the portfolio is presented. These two tables can be used for summative or end-of-course presentations. Sample scoring rubrics for portfolios are also found in Chapter 4 and on the CD.

Table 6.6B provides a sample of how a particular presentation was rated by a teacher credential candidate's peers.

Summary

This chapter discussed how to prepare and develop the portfolio for presentation. Some presentation strategies and suggestions for scoring were offered.

Table 6.6A Sample Scoring Rubric for Portfolio Presentation

Below Standard	X	*Meets Standard*	X	*Exceeds Standard*	X
• Presents a limited picture of candidate. • Presents some evidence of competencies in standards presented. • Does not highlight strengths. • Takes more than allotted time for the presentation. • Presentation is communicated to the audience with some difficulty. • Little evidence of reflective engagement.		• Presents overall picture of candidate. • Presents adequate evidence of competencies in standards presented. • Highlights strengths. • Adequately uses allotted time for the presentation. • Presentation is clearly communicated to the audience. • Evidence of reflective engagement.		• Presents overall picture of candidate. • Exceeds in all standards presented. • Highlights strengths. • Adequately uses the allotted time for the presentation. • Presentation is engaging and clearly communicated to the audience. • Substantial-quality evidence of reflective engagement.	

Overall score:

Below Standard **Meets Standard** **Exceeds Standard**

Comments:

The portfolio presentation should be focused and provide evidence of professional competencies in national, state, and/or local professional standards. The portfolio contents must be organized for ease of presentation. Candidates need guidelines, opportunities to practice, and critiques of their presentation. Presentations should be guided by whether the portfolios are being presented at the preservice, job-interview, or professional-development levels and also by whether the portfolios are formative or summative. This chapter mainly focused on program summative presentations but provided suggestions for formative presentations, such as portfolio conferencing.

Candidates need to retool their portfolios for presentation and check for understanding regarding the expectations for the presentation. The audience and the type of setting for the presentation should determine the most

Table 6.6B Sample Scoring Rubric for Portfolio Presentation

METHODS AND ACTIVITIES PRESENTATION
PEER EVALUATIONS

Presentation of The Very Hungry Caterpillar *using the natural approach.*

Percentage rankings, where 1 is *Very High,* and 5 is *Needs Improvement.*

	1	2	3	4	5
Clarity of Objectives	38%	46%	0%	8%	8%
ELD1	67%	23%	0%	5%	5%
ELD2	58%	32%	5%	5%	0%
ELD3	71%	24%	0%	5%	0%
ELD4	63%	32%	0%	5%	0%
ELD5	67%	23%	5%	5%	0%
Student Involvement	82%	9%	9%	0%	0%
General Appeal	68%	23%	9%	0%	0%
Used Lang-Arts Strats	69%	22%	9%	0%	0%

Presentation Strengths

Visuals such as real fruit and pictures of different types of caterpillars.

Book (pictures), worksheet handout.

Got everyone involved.

Nice job of bringing closure to the lesson.

Visual aids.

Good incorporation of content with math, days of the week, vocabulary.

Realia, days, charts, throwing fruit, good teamwork, nice review, yummy salad. Student involvement, worksheet for reinforcement.

YUM!

Great visuals, allowed for involvement.

Energy, organization.

Being able to see the actual fruit and writing the answers on the board really helped the ELD1 students.

Clever way to determine participation—throwing fruit.

Vocabulary.

Nicely articulated, good presentation of the book.

Very smooth and confident delivery. You both appeared to be trained, professional teachers.

Good presentation.

Good voice.

Student interaction, presentation.

Fruit salad given to students connected with lesson.

Range of activities, clear presentation, yummy fruit salad.

Loved how you connected real foods with the book.

Suggestions/Recommendations Move at a slightly faster pace to accommodate all students. Show more pictures of stages of butterfly. Didn't help us understand healthy vs. unhealthy. Repeat words in English, as well. Point to objects in picture. Have students repeat repetitious sections of book in unison, e.g., "But he was still hungry." Good, you did this! You were beautiful! Don't change a thing! Having some of the ELD4 and ELD5 students write the information on the chart. Explain terms, e.g., "real" vs. "imaginary" Could be more fluently presented. No recommendations. I thought it went very well. How do you teach them "adding"? Lesson was good, but maybe wait to give the fruit salad last. More (bigger) pictures/visuals; anyhow, great job. Some words are a bit too complicated for ELD1–2 students.
Additional Comments/Ideas I liked the way you incorporated math into the activity. Good job! Especially going at it first. *May be too easy for ELD5 students; they might lose interest in the topic. Overall, great presentation.* *Nice attention-getter with "fruit throwing."* Good modeling with worksheet. Somewhat abstract for earlier levels, though the fruit helped. Get it out, dramatize. Good pictures to reinforce stories. What is healthy? Great presentation. You incorporated science, literacy, and math. Clever tying story to concrete fruit. Nice having class count together. Good gestures. Susan: nice gestures, voice, presentation of story. Great lesson! First part ran a little slow, but I'm sure with practice you'll be better. Thanks for the fruit. Very well-prepared materially. Overall, a great presentation.

appropriate container for the presentation. Tips for scheduling presentations were discussed. If portfolio presentations will include a variety of audiences, it is essential to engage in long-range planning. One may choose from a variety of presentation formats and schedules, including presentations to a whole class or group of colleagues, presentations in small groups over several days, and presentations in small groups in one time period. Presentation formats will vary depending on goals, purposes, and the time frame.

For Further Reading

Winsor, P., & Ellefson, B. (1998, Winter). Professional portfolios in teacher education: An exploration of their value and potential. *Teacher Education Quarterly*, pp. 68–81.

7

Electronic Portfolios

I hear and I forget, I see and remember, I do and I understand.

—Confucius

Chapter Objectives

Readers will be able to

- organize artifacts into folders,
- name artifacts using naming conventions,
- create an electronic portfolio using Microsoft Word,
- create a Web-based portfolio using Microsoft Word,
- create an electronic portfolio using Microsoft PowerPoint,
- create a Web-based portfolio using Microsoft PowerPoint.

Scenario

Greg is working on his elementary teaching credential and is faced with preparing his electronic portfolio. His friend Rachel is working on her single-subject secondary teaching credential and is also faced with preparing her electronic portfolio. Rachel is quite familiar with Microsoft PowerPoint and has decided to create hers using that tool. Greg is more familiar with Microsoft Word and opts to use that instead. Both are making their portfolios CD-based but also want to be able to eventually post them on the Web.

Greg voiced his concerns about the project to Rachel: "I know I'm going to make my portfolio in Word and present it on a CD, but I also want to eventually put it online. Will I be able to do that without having to make two portfolios?"

Rachel had seen online portfolios that used PowerPoint. "I know I can use PowerPoint to make a Web-based portfolio, but I'm not sure if I want to post it online. I would prefer to have mine on a CD that I can bring to an interview and give to the principal.

Overview

Both students in the scenario will be able to do what they want to do using their chosen tool. Both Microsoft Word and PowerPoint are good tools for creating an electronic portfolio, and both of them can then convert those portfolios into a Web-based portfolio.

This chapter lists the benefits of electronic portfolios and tells when and where to use them. Then it takes the reader step-by-step through the creation of an electronic portfolio using four methods:

1. The first method uses Word; it is CD-based and requires Word to view the portfolio. This entry-level format would be appropriate for candidates who are familiar with word processing and have entry-level file management skills.

2. The second method also uses Word; it is Web-based (however, this can also be CD-based) and is viewed using a Web browser (e.g., Internet Explorer, Netscape, Safari). This middle-level format would be appropriate for candidates who are familiar with word processing and have entry- to middle-level file management skills.

3. The third method uses PowerPoint; it is viewed as a slide show and requires PowerPoint to view the portfolio. The requirement of having PowerPoint to view the portfolio can be averted by using the Pack and Go feature. This feature includes a PowerPoint player, which allows the portfolio to be viewed on computers that do not have PowerPoint installed. This entry-level format would be appropriate for candidates who are familiar with PowerPoint and have entry-level file management skills.

4. The fourth method again uses PowerPoint; it is Web-based (this can also be CD-based) and is viewed using a Web browser. This middle-level format is appropriate for candidates who are familiar with PowerPoint and have entry- to middle-level file management skills.

Remember that electronic portfolios created for the Web need not be uploaded onto a server to be viewed. They can be viewed from a CD using a Web browser.

Benefits of Electronic Portfolios

Portfolios traditionally have housed a myriad of artifacts, which are often stored in binders. The portfolio can become extremely cumbersome, however, with the addition of more and more videos, pictures, audiotapes, CDs, and papers. As these artifacts are collected, the binders keep growing in both width and number. Because the majority of written artifacts in a portfolio have been created digitally, the text is basically ready to format into an electronic portfolio. Any other artifacts to be included can also be digitized, either personally or professionally. Once digitized, these are ready to be organized into an electronic portfolio.

Portfolios can be stored on a computer hard drive, a portable mass storage device (flash drive, Zip disk, USB mini hard drive), a CD, a DVD, a commercial Web site, an educational Web site, or any combination of these. The method of storage is determined by the intended method of presentation. A word of caution, however: No matter what media you decide on for electronic portfolio storage, always, always, always have another copy as a backup. For example, a CD left in the car can warp and become unusable. A Web-based server could crash, and although we hate to even think of it, your hard drive could crash, too.

Electronic portfolios are often works in progress instead of finished products. This is especially true as candidates prepare their portfolios for credential or certification programs. New artifacts can be added as coursework is completed and standards are addressed without having to worry if the contents will fit their present binder. An electronic portfolio should therefore be thought of as a living document that chronicles the ongoing work of teacher candidates.

The creation and use of electronic portfolios also brings into practice the National Educational Technology Standards (NETS) Standard 5 (Productivity and Professional Practice), which recognizes that teachers use technology to enhance their productivity and professional practice. The NETS 5 states that teachers

- use technology resources to engage in ongoing professional development and lifelong learning;
- continually evaluate and reflect on professional practice to make informed decisions regarding the use of technology in support of student learning;

- apply technology to increase productivity;
- use technology to communicate and collaborate with peers, parents, and the larger community in order to nurture student learning.

Many candidates are initially intimidated by the technologies used in creating the portfolios. But after completing their work, they usually see the usefulness of the portfolio, as well as the need to bring technology into their future classrooms (Wright, Stallworth, & Ray, 2002).

The most important feature of electronic portfolios is the ability to link artifacts to the standards that they address. In addition, electronic portfolios give one the ability to link a single element that satisfies multiple standards to each of those standards without having to make multiple copies of the information. For example, if a teacher candidate creates a lesson that addresses three standards, electronic portfolios allow links to the same lesson from each of the three standards without having to create three copies of the lesson. Also, there can be links to each of the three standards that are covered from the single lesson. Electronic portfolios easily incorporate multidirectional links that solve complex navigational and organizational problems. The only disadvantage is the need to have a computer to view an electronic portfolio.

When, Where, and How to Use

Portfolios in one form or another are being used in about 90 percent of schools, colleges, and departments of education as decision-making tools for standards-based decisions regarding certification or licensure (Wilkerson & Lang, 2003). These same portfolios can then be used to show future employers what the candidate is capable of.

CD or Web-based, which portfolio is right for me? Some schools of education currently offer students space on school servers for Web-based portfolios. Other schools have contracts with commercial vendors that handle Web-based portfolios (Figure 7.1), such as TaskStream (www.taskstream.com) or FolioLive (www.foliolive.com). Candidates can then store their portfolios on the school or commercial servers and give prospective employers a Web address to view their portfolios at any time. These sites are password protected. Guest IDs and passwords can be created or are provided to allow access to the portfolio for prospective employers. Candidates generally need some instruction or training in order to post a portfolio on a commercial site. If school-server and commercial-vendor options are not available,

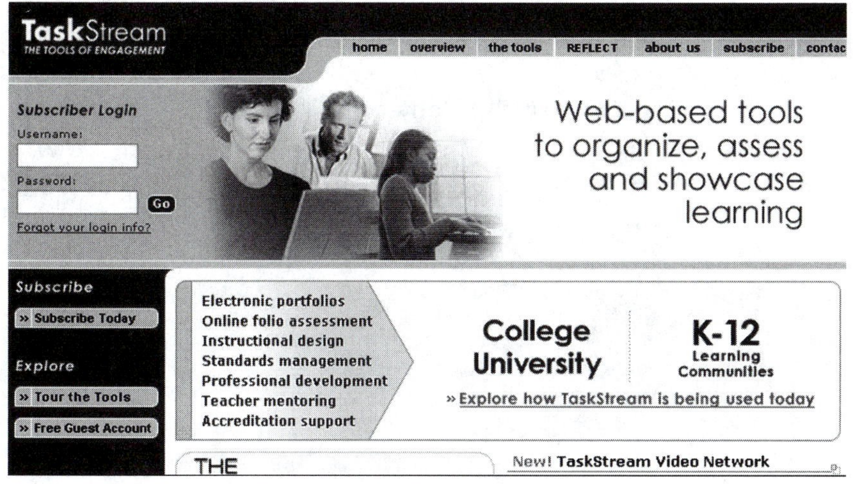

Figure 7.1 TaskStream: A Commercial Web-Based Portfolio Presentation Site

there are alternatives. For example, a CD version of an electronic portfolio is very versatile. Copies can easily be made for each prospective employer.

When CDs are used to store an electronic portfolio, there are options for its presentation. PowerPoint can be used to create an electronic portfolio, especially one with a number of videos, audio selections, and pictures. The PowerPoint-based portfolio can be presented using PowerPoint, or it can be converted to HTML (hypertext markup language) and be presented using a Web browser (see Table 7.1). Just because a portfolio is Web-based doesn't mean it has to be on the Web. The portfolio can be burned onto a CD and viewed from the CD. An advantage of having a portfolio on a CD is that the prospective employer needs access only to a computer, not to the Internet itself.

Microsoft Word is often used as an electronic portfolio creation tool. Because many students already employ Word to word process, they feel comfortable using it. Like in the process of using PowerPoint, one can create electronic portfolios in Word that can be presented either in Word or by converting Word to HTML and then viewing the portfolio using a Web browser (Table 7.2). Also, like the PowerPoint electronic portfolios, the Word electronic portfolios can be burned onto a CD.

Table 7.1 Table of Contents Shown in PowerPoint (A) and in HTML (B)

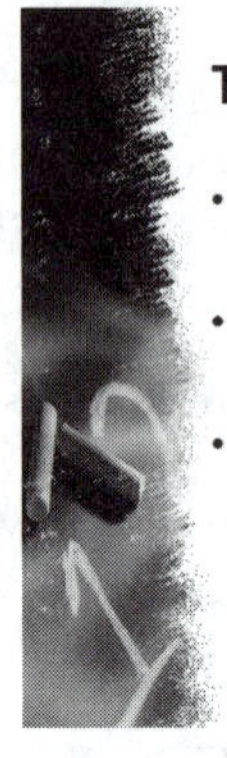

A. Sample of a table of contents from an electronic portfolio presented in PowerPoint

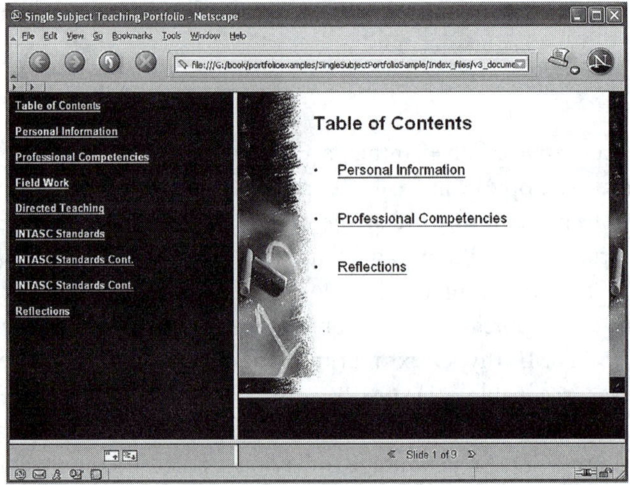

B. Sample of the same table of contents converted to HTML and presented in Netscape

Posting an electronic portfolio on the Web, or burning it onto a CD to be left with prospective employers, allows employers to view candidates' work either with candidates present or after they have left. Leaving a CD or a Web address is especially important if there is no time or equipment available during the interview to view the portfolio.

Table 7.2 Table of Contents Shown in Word (A) and in HTML (B)

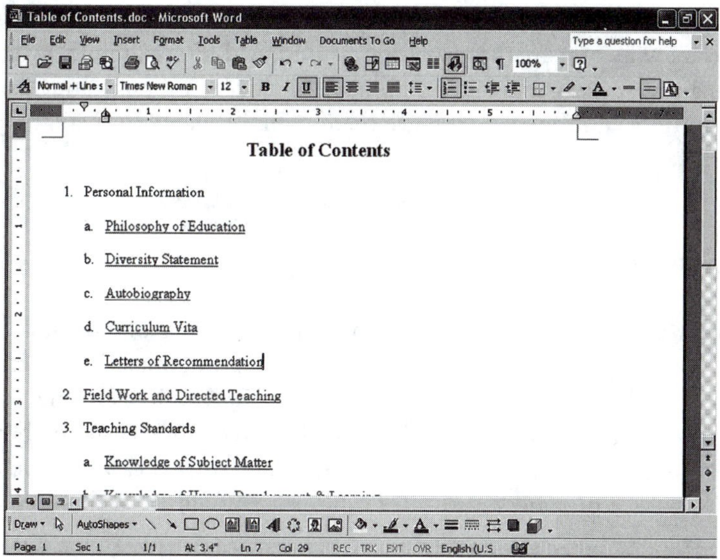

A. Sample of a table of contents from an electronic portfolio presented in Word

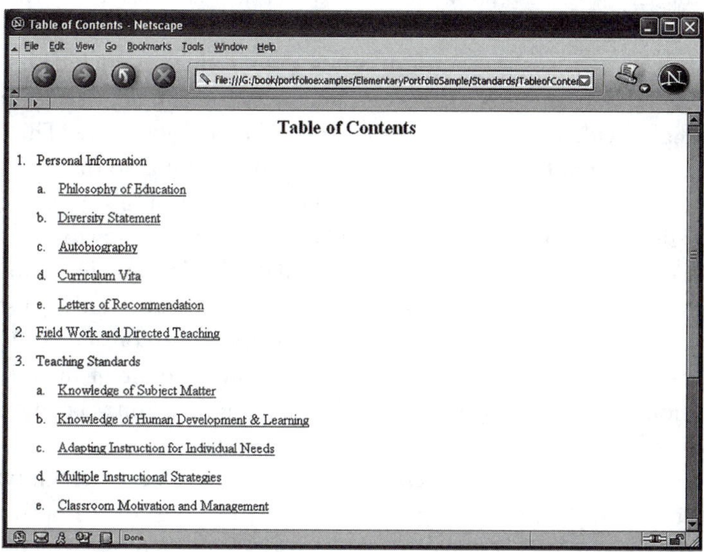

B. Sample of the same table of contents converted to HTML and presented in Netscape

In this age of identity theft, candidates need to pay special attention to a few parts of the Web-based portfolio. Before posting a portfolio live on the Web (unless it is password-protected), you need to pay special attention to the way personal information is presented. For example, instead of showing an address and phone number, include an e-mail address. And instead of listing references, replace them with, "References available upon request."

Storage Options

Although the most popular storage method is posting or uploading electronic portfolios to the Web, there are other storage options (Figure 7.2). To use the method of Web storage, a Web site must be available. Some schools offer this service, and some Web sites offer free storage space (but you usually have to put up with ad banners), or Web space can be purchased. Internet service providers also offer a limited amount of Web space along with a regular subscription.

Instead of the Web-based method of electronic portfolio storage, however, one can use the popular and inexpensive method of burning a portfolio onto a CD. CDs are very inexpensive, and even if the equipment to create the CD is not available at home or work, many photocopying businesses offer CD-burning services. A CD holds 700 megabytes of information. That is a lot of information unless digital video is included. Digital video eats up storage space extremely quickly. For example, twenty minutes of raw digital video can take up to 3 gigabytes of storage space. This digital video can be formatted using a variety of video programs so that the twenty minutes can fit on a CD and up to two hours can fit on a DVD. If quite a bit of digital video is included, a DVD is a good alternative storage media. If a DVD is chosen for storage, make sure that a DVD-capable computer or player is available for the portfolio presentation. As an alternative, a second, CD-based version of the electronic portfolio should be considered. On this version, either omit the digital video or limit the amount of digital video. This option is a good backup in case DVD capabilities cannot be met for the required viewing.

"I know how to store my electronic portfolio once I'm done, but what do I store it on while I'm working on it? It's just too big for a floppy disk!" There are various storage options. A Zip drive in a computer at home or at school is one solution. Zip disks come in 100-, 250-, and 750-megabyte sizes. Another option is a flash drive. Flash drives or pen drives come in a range of sizes from 64 megabytes to 2 gigabytes. There are also miniature

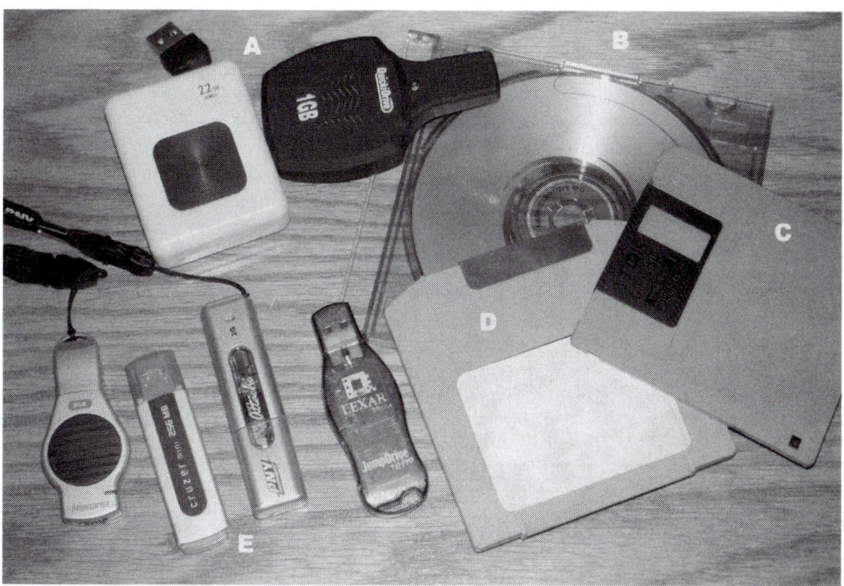

Figure 7.2 Storage Devices

Clockwise from top left: (A) two types of USB mini hard drives, (B) CD, (C) floppy disk, (D) Zip disk, and (E) four types of flash drives.

hard drives (Figure 7.2) that come in a range of sizes. Table 7.3 presents a storage-device comparison chart.

The flash drives and mini hard drives plug into the USB port on any Windows computer running Windows 98 second edition (SE) or above, or on a Macintosh system 9 or above. Windows 98SE requires drivers to be installed, but the other operating systems need no additional software. These drives are getting fairly inexpensive and are very easy to carry. They fit right into a pocket or purse with no problem. Many also come with an attachable neck strap. The only problem with these devices is forgetting to disconnect them from the computer! Portable mass-storage devices allow candidates to keep a copy of their portfolio handy without lugging around a laptop. But beware! Always have a backup copy—it doesn't hurt to have two. If one gets lost or corrupted, starting from a backup is always easier than starting over.

Creating an Electronic Portfolio

There are some important steps to follow in creating an electronic portfolio. Gathering and preparing the files can be tedious, but doing this task carefully

Table 7.3 Storage-Device Comparison Chart

Device	*Capacity*	*Comparison*
3½" floppy	1.44 megabytes	360,000–1,440,000 characters
Zip disk	100 megabytes	70 floppies
CD-ROM	640 megabytes	445 floppies
Flash drive	128 megabytes	88 floppies
Flash drive	512 megabytes	356 floppies
Flash drive	1 gigabyte	711 floppies
DVD	4.7 gigabytes	3,342 floppies

will avoid many problems. Pay special attention to file names and folder names. A little time and effort at the beginning stages will help you avoid many hours of troubleshooting and repairing links that do not work.

Getting Started—Naming Files

Naming files and folders has always been easy to do on a Mac and is equally easy now with a Windows machine. Also, changing the name of a file or folder is not a difficult task. Just as important as collecting the evidence for a portfolio is making sure that some simple naming rules are followed.

Yes, it is acceptable and quite common to use multiword file names (e.g., Table of Contents.doc). However, this is not a good practice for portfolio files that *will* be used or even *might* be used in an electronic portfolio that will be posted on the Web. Mac and Windows servers don't seem to mind multiple-word file names, but Unix servers have a problem with them. The problem is that every time the server comes across a space, it inserts "%20." So if the file name is "Standard 1 lesson," it will be read as "Standard% 201%20lesson." And because the two phrases don't match, any link to that file won't work.

So instead of naming the file "Standard 1 lesson," name the file "Standard_1_lesson" or "Standard1lesson." The use of the underscore (_) instead of a space is a safe alternative, as is just removing the spaces and running the words together using no spacing. It doesn't seem to matter if the file names are long, if they are one-word file names or use the underscore between words. Take the time to make sure that all file and folder names conform to this rule and rename text, audio, video, and graphic files as needed.

For example, use Windows Explorer or My Computer to look at file and folder names. If any of the files names use multiple words, rename them. The folders and file names in Table 7.4A include multiword names. All of these folders and files must be renamed, making sure that all spaces are removed (or replaced by an underscore). Table 7.4B shows the file and folders as seen in Windows Explorer after being renamed. To rename a file or folder, right click (for a PC) on it and choose Rename. Then type the new name and press Enter. Make sure to check each file and folder as it is selected for use in the portfolio.

Organizing Files

Organization and presentation are two key elements in electronic portfolios. Before creating an electronic portfolio, organization is the crucial step. Portfolios are living documents, so the process of file collection and organization is a central step in achieving an error-free portfolio. Start by creating a folder for your portfolio and name it "Portfolio," or something similar. In Chapter 5, there are sample tables of contents. Create a draft table of contents using Word. After it is created, save this file inside the created Portfolio folder.

The contents of the table of contents will determine how many folders are needed and what they will be named. Create subfolders inside the Portfolio folder for each topic in your table of contents. To help organize the files, store all the artifacts for each topic in its corresponding folders. This will help in organizing the files. All folders and files used in the portfolio must be contained in the main Portfolio folder. In Table 7.4B, there is a listing of the folders created for an elementary teaching portfolio as seen in Windows Explorer. Notice that there are folders for each main category and that everything is located within the folder called "ElementaryPortfolioSample."

Once the folders have been created, add each piece of evidence in its appropriate folder (remember, don't forget to check the file names and remove any spaces). The artifacts files to be added inside the folders would be the Word documents that have been created (i.e., lesson plans, student teaching logs, etc.) Don't be afraid to create folders within a folder to help you in the organization of files.

All files, except for the file that starts the electronic portfolio and the table of contents, are kept within a folder inside the main Portfolio folder. This

Table 7.4 Multiword Names (A) and Single-Word Names (B)

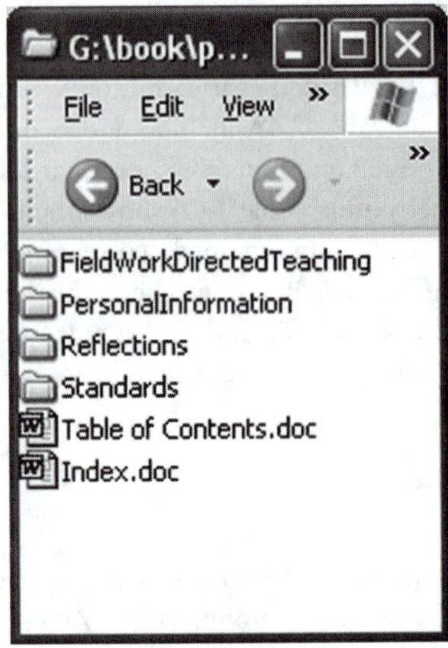

A. Multiword folders and files viewed using My Computer

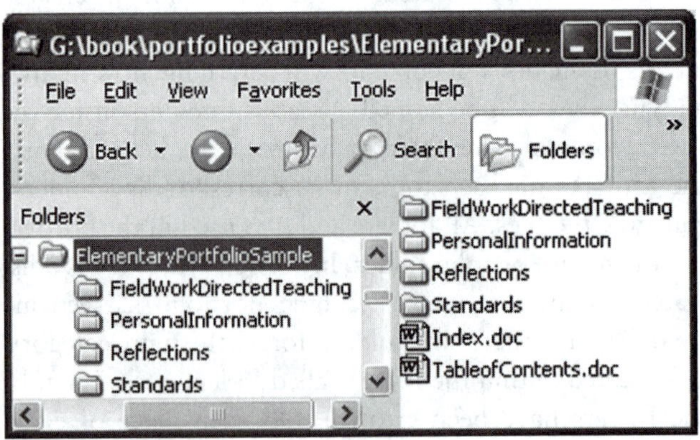

B. Renamed single-word folders and files viewed using Windows Explorer

starting file would be your opening page, and it is named "Index." This organization makes it easy for the viewer, perhaps a potential employer, to access the portfolio without having to guess which of the thirty or so files should be opened first. Many employers don't have the time to search for this information.

Look at the table of contents (TOC) for an elementary credential portfolio in Table 7.5. Each main topic heading has a separate folder that will

Table 7.5 Elementary Credential TOC and Corresponding Folder Structure

Elementary Credential Table of Contents	*Corresponding Folder Structure*
1. Personal Information a. Philosophy of Education b. Philosophy of Classroom Management c. Diversity Statement d. Resume e. Application to XYZ School District f. Transcripts g. References/Letters of Recommendation h. Exams	PersonalInformation
2. Fieldwork and Directed Teaching	FieldWorkDirectedTeaching
3. Teaching Standards a. Knowledge of Subject Matter b. Knowledge of Human Development and Learning c. Adapting Instruction for Individual Needs d. Multiple Instructional Strategies e. Classroom Motivation and Management f. Communication Skills g. Instructional Planning Skills h. Assessment of Student Learning i. Professional Commitment and Responsibility j. Partnerships	Standards
4. Reflections	Reflections

Table 7.6 Elementary Credential Folder and Artifacts Within the Folder

Folder	Artifacts (files) contained within the folder
PersonalInformation	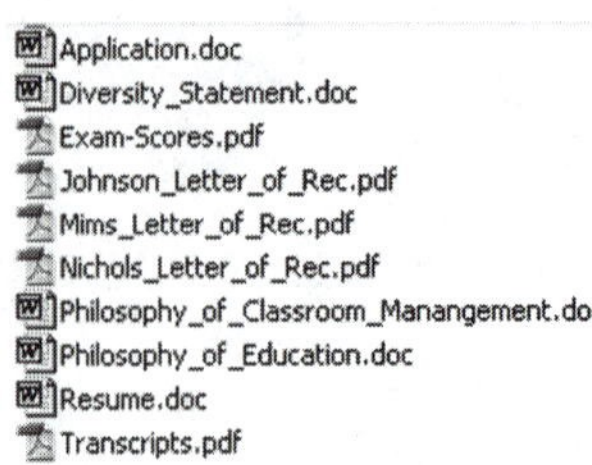 Application.doc Diversity_Statement.doc Exam-Scores.pdf Johnson_Letter_of_Rec.pdf Mims_Letter_of_Rec.pdf Nichols_Letter_of_Rec.pdf Philosophy_of_Classroom_Manangement.doc Philosophy_of_Education.doc Resume.doc Transcripts.pdf

house the artifacts for that topic. Table 7.6 shows one of the folders and some of the files that would be stored within it. Table 7.7 shows the TOC for a single-subject credential portfolio.

Portfolios need to be kept up-to-date. Folders that correspond to the table of contents allow the candidate to add new evidence or find existing evidence for edits or other uses. Don't be afraid to add more subfolders to help keep artifacts organized. For instance, suppose there is a lesson plan on mammals that has five different files: the lesson plan, four worksheets, and a PowerPoint presentation. To keep all these files together, create a subfolder called "MammalsLessonPlan" inside the TeachingStandards folder. With all five files stored inside this subfolder, there is less risk of losing track of one of the files.

Handling Nondigital Artifacts

"I can't find the file for this great activity, but I do have a paper copy of it. Can I still use it for my electronic portfolio?" Yes! Access to a scanner and Adobe Acrobat writer (www.adobe.com) or CutePDF (www.cutepdf.com) will allow you to scan the document and save it as a PDF (Portable Document Format) file. Adobe Acrobat writer is the standard for creating PDF files. Adobe offers a very reasonable discounted education price for educators. An alternative is CutePDF, which has a free version that can be downloaded. It doesn't have all the bells and whistles like Adobe Acrobat writer, but it works well. For instance, Adobe Acrobat writer allows multiple pages to be scanned into a single PDF document, regardless of the scanning software being used. When using CutePDF, however, the scanning software must be able to scan multiple

Table 7.7 Single Subject Credential TOC and Corresponding Folder Structure

Single Subject Credential Table of Contents	*Corresponding Folder Structure*
1. Personal Information a. Philosophy of Education b. Diversity Statement c. Autobiography d. Curriculum Vitae	PersonalInformation
2. Teaching Standards a. Knowledge of Subject Matter b. Knowledge of Human Development and Learning c. Adapting Instruction for Individual Needs d. Multiple Instructional Strategies e. Classroom Motivation and Management f. Communication Skills g. Instructional Planning Skills h. Assessment of Student Learning i. Professional Commitment and Responsibility j. Partnerships	TeachingStandards
3. Fieldwork and Directed Teaching	FieldworkDirectedTeaching
4. Reflections	Reflections
5. Exams	Exams

pages into a single file. Then the file is printed to CutePDF to convert it to a PDF file. PDF files can be viewed using Adobe Acrobat reader, which is a free download at the Adobe Web site.

Converting a document into a PDF file is as simple as printing the document:

1. Choose File.
2. Then choose Print, and on the print menu click the down arrow to the right of Printer Name.
3. Next, choose CutePDF or Adobe Acrobat writer (Figure 7.3).
4. Next, the Name File dialog box will appear.
5. Name the file and save it in a folder.

The document has now been converted to a PDF file.

Other examples of nondigital media are letters of recommendation, certificates, credentials, and standardized test scores. All of these various documents need to be scanned to digitize them. However, converting scanned documents to graphics files (e.g., with the extensions .jpg, .jpeg, .tif, or .tiff) is not recommended. For instance, Greg in our scenario wants to include a copy of his credential. So he scans it and saves it as a JPG and includes it in the portfolio. But, in order to fit it in his document, it needed to be sized down. Unfortunately, when he tries to view it, the credential is so small it is virtually unreadable. The answer to this dilemma is saving the scanned document as a PDF file. With a PDF file, if the document is too small, one can use the zoom feature to increase the size so that the document is legible (Figure 7.4). The PDF format is good for certificates, credentials, awards, letters of recommendation, test score documentation, seating charts, and so forth.

Still pictures can be scanned using a scanner and a graphics program, such as Adobe Photoshop, Adobe Photoshop Elements, Microsoft Picture It! Photo, or Jasc Paint Shop Pro. Pictures should be saved in the JPG or JPEG format, which is the standard for photographs. When scanning images, some people save images in the TIFF format, which is great for archival files because it saves a lot of detail. This format is also very large. Unless the images are for archival storage, JPG format works well for images. Once they are scanned, the images can be inserted into a Word document, PowerPoint slide show, or HTML page.

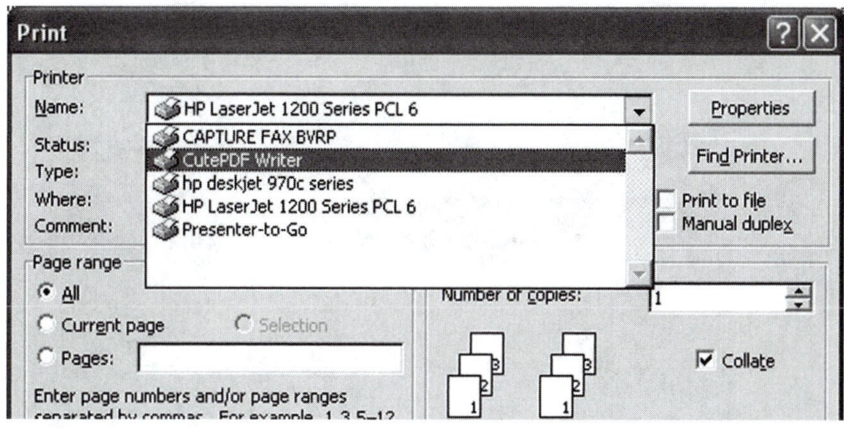

Figure 7.3 The Word Print Dialog Box

Click the down arrow to the right of Printer Name: and choose CutePDF instead of a printer. This will convert a Word document file into a PDF file.

Many video cameras are digital and can be connected to a computer through a video capture card and a video editing program (e.g., Adobe Premiere, Adobe Premiere Elements, Pinnacle Studio) If your video is not digital, there are video capture cards that digitize the video as it is captured (www.pinnaclesys.com). Some photo stores will also digitize video. Once digitized and edited, this video can be inserted into Word or PowerPoint. A number of online tutorials address this specific issue. Good places to start are www.lynda.com or www.atomiclearning.com, both of which are subscription sites but also have some free tutorials available.

Creating the Opening Page and Table of Contents in Word

In our scenario, Greg, the elementary credential candidate, preferred using Word to create his electronic portfolio. Here is how he would do that.

The opening page is like a first impression. Make it a good one! It shouldn't be too fancy; just clean and to the point. It should have your name, the date of the last revision, and maybe the logo of your school or some other supportive graphic. This page may be left white or have a background added. Table 7.8 shows an example of an opening page without and with 

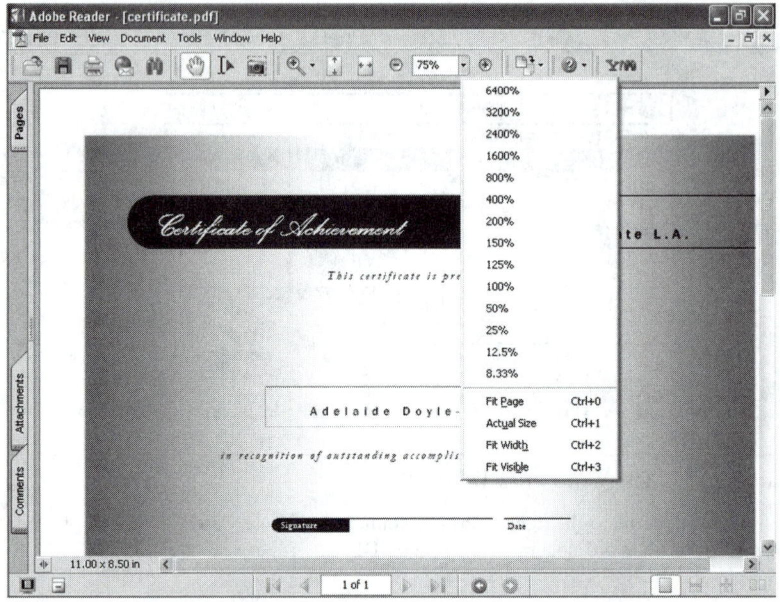

Figure 7.4 Sample of Certificate of Achievement as Viewed in Adobe Acrobat Reader

This is viewed at 75 percent but can be enlarged if needed.

a background. The opening page will have a link to the table of contents. Once the opening page is created, save it in the main Portfolio folder that you created. The opening file is called "Index.doc." Index.doc and the table of contents should be the only files not in a subfolder. Remember, don't use spaces in file or folder names.

Backgrounds can be very effective or very distracting, depending on how they are used. Make sure that the text is easy to read and that the background is pleasing to the eyes. To insert a background in Word,

1. Click on Format
2. Then on Background
3. Then Fill Effects

The Fill Effects dialog box will open. The options for the background include gradients (Table 7.9A), textures (Table 7.9B), patterns, and pictures. On the gradients tab, a single color, two colors, or preset colors can be used

Table 7.8 Index File Shown With No Background (A) and With Background (B)

Elementary Teaching Credential

Portfolio

of

Greg Nichols

(Click on title to enter)

June 25, 2005

A. Without background

Elementary Teaching Credential

Portfolio

of

Greg Nichols

(Click on title to enter)

June 25, 2005

B. With background

Table 7.9 Fill-Effects Gradient Tab (A) and Texture Tab (B)

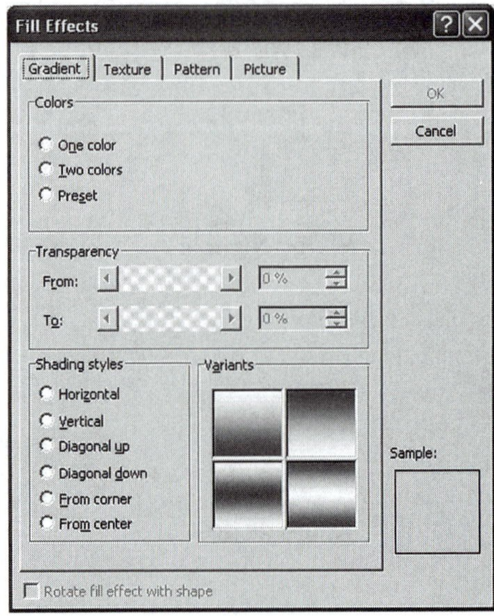

A. Fill effects dialog box open to the Gradient Tab

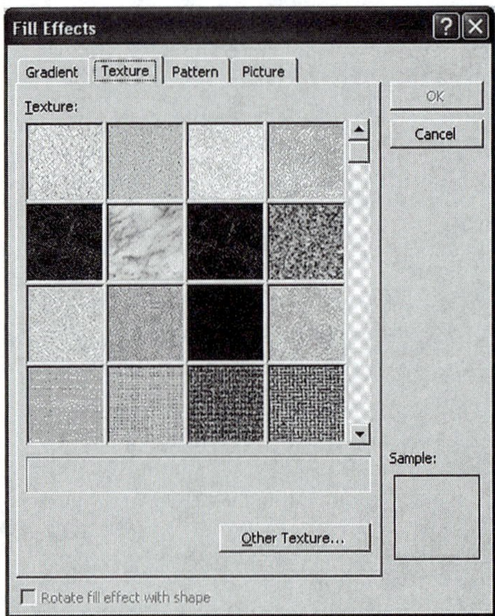

B. Fill effects dialog box open to the Texture Tab

in a variety of shading styles. The direction of the gradient and the transparency can also be changed. These are simple and effective backgrounds. There is also a good choice of textures on the Texture tab. If Word doesn't have a texture or picture to meet your needs, pictures, photographs, or additional graphics can be imported. In the case of Table 7.8B, a texture called Canvas was chosen. It is important to remember, when using any type of background, to make sure that the text is clearly visible and not obscured by the background. A page with a plain white background is much better than a page with a great background that has unreadable text.

Earlier, we discussed creating the table of contents page (see Chapter 5). This page will act as the navigation page for the portfolio. It will look similar to a table of contents page in a book, except there will be no page numbers. Instead, each topic will be hyperlinked to the supporting documents. Save this file in the main Portfolio folder, and name it "Tableof Contents.doc."

Word or HTML—Which One Is Right for Me?

The main difference between a Word document and a Word document converted to HTML is the way in which the file is viewed. A Word document is viewed in Word or is printed out on a printer. A Word document converted to HTML is viewed in a Web browser (e.g., Netscape, Internet Explorer, Safari). A Web browser is used whether the files are uploaded to the Web or saved on a CD, a hard drive, or any other large-capacity storage device. An HTML file does not have to be uploaded to the Web but can be if there is Web space is available.

When viewing a portfolio in Word, to follow a link the user must hold down the Control (Ctrl) key as the link is clicked and a new Word document is opened. So if the user clicks on fourteen different links, then fourteen different documents are opened at the same time. In HTML, the user clicks on the link (without having to hold the Ctrl key) and it opens the next page in the same window, not a new one. So if the user clicks on fourteen different links, there will still be only one browser window open. The user is also able to review previously viewed pages by clicking on the Back button on the browser. Both formats are acceptable, although the Web-based portfolio is more portable.

If the portfolio is going to be Web-based (uploaded to the Web or not), continue with this section. If your portfolio is going to be Word-based, skip this section and go to the section on creating links.

Converting Word Files to HTML

To preserve the original electronic portfolio, a copy should be made. It is strongly suggested that the copy, rather than the original, be converted to HTML. All Word files need to be converted to HTML, but the PDF files do not.

To convert a Word file to HTML, follow these steps:

1. Click on File.
2. Save as Web Page (Figure 7.5).
3. A Save As dialog box will open (Figure 7.6).
4. Each file should have a very short descriptive title—this is *not* the file name. The title is what is shown on the very top of the Web browser as each page is viewed. Click on the Change Title button to add a title (Figure 7.6). For instance, the opening page title would most likely be "Elementary Teaching Credential Portfolio" or "[Your Name]'s Portfolio."
5. After giving the page a title, click OK.
6. Before the file is saved (i.e., converted), make sure that the file will be saved in the correct folder.
7. Check the "Save in:" folder and make sure it is your main Portfolio folder (Figure 7.6).
8. Then click Save.

Word creates an HTML file, as well as a folder with all the necessary files to have this page viewed online. Not all files require Word to create folders. If there are any backgrounds or images, Word puts a copy of these files in a folder. These files must be available for the documents to be viewed correctly using a Web browser. Don't erase them, or it will not work! Just be aware that you will have a new folder for some of the Word files that were converted to HTML. Save each of the files in their original folders. For instance, if there is an artifact called "Organized1.doc" saved in the TeachingStandards folder, then when it is saved as HTML it should again be saved in the TeachingStandards folder. Thus, a new file named "Organized1.htm" (and, if needed, a new folder called "Organized1_files") will be created by Word and saved in the TeachingStandards folder.

This same sequence needs to be completed for all of the Word documents in your portfolio (for converting PowerPoint files, see the section on PowerPoint, which follows). Just be sure to check the folder that is listed next to "Save in:" to make sure that it is correct.

Once all the files have been converted to HTML, the files are ready to be linked. If the links are created before the files are converted, problems

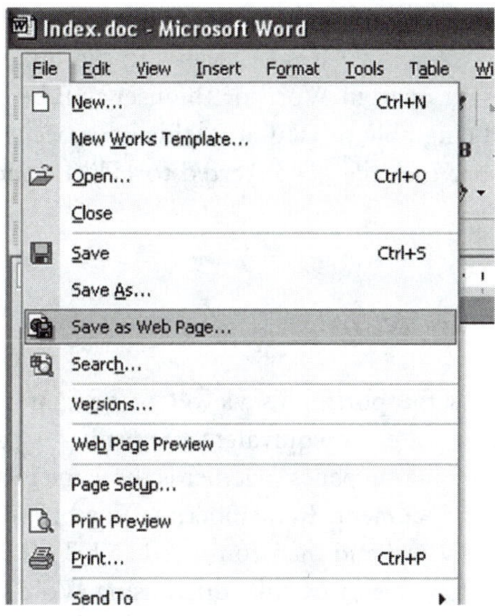

Figure 7.5 Menu Option to Convert a Word Document to HTML

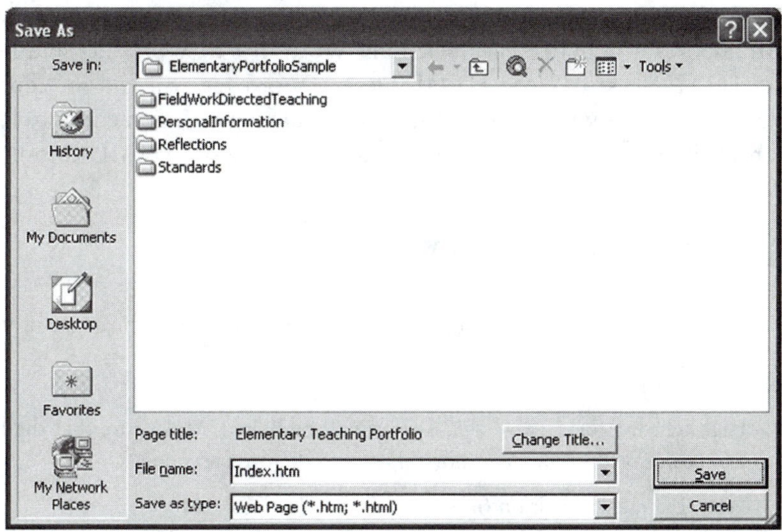

Figure 7.6 The Save As HTML Dialog Box in Word

The page title is "Single Subject Teaching Credential." This can be changed by clicking on the Change Title button. This file will be saved in the ElementaryPortfolioSample folder. This location can be changed by clicking the down arrow to the right of "Save in:" and then navigating to the correct folder.

will occur. Instead of linking to another Web page, it will be linked to a Word document. That is, instead of viewing the linked page in a Web browser, the link will open in Word or the user will be prompted to save the file instead of being able to view it. If this does occur, the error can be fixed by making sure that file is converted to HTML and editing the link to the file.

Creating Links in Word

Creating links allows the portfolio's viewer to navigate through the electronic portfolio. Links are the equivalent of turning a page or using tabs on a paper portfolio. Linking pages together is the same in a Word document and a Word HTML document. Remember, a Word HTML document is a document created in Word and then converted to HTML. Even though it is viewed using a Web browser, it is still edited using Word. It is important to note the following, however: If the file is double clicked on to Edit, it will not open Word, but it will open a Web browser. So to edit Word HTML documents, first open Word, then click on File and Open and navigate to the file to be edited. Another alternative is to right click on the file and choose Open With, then choose Word.

An important note to remember: Link Word files to Word files and link Word HTML files to Word HTML files. A Word file will end in ".doc"; a Word HTML file will end in ".htm." The following are instructions to link files regardless of whether they are Word (.doc) or Word HTML (.htm).

Linking Word and Word HTML Files

To create a link from the opening page (Index file) to the Tableof Contents file, follow these steps:

1. Highlight the text (Table 7.10A) that will be linked. Make sure that the file has been saved in the main portfolio folder before creating a link.
2. From the menu, click on Insert.
3. Hyperlink (Table 7.10B).
4. The Insert Hyperlink dialog box will open (Figure 7.7).
5. In the "Link to:" column, the Existing File or Web Page should be selected.
6. In the "Look in:" column, the Current Folder should be selected.

Table 7.10 Selecting Text (A) and Inserting Hyperlink (B)

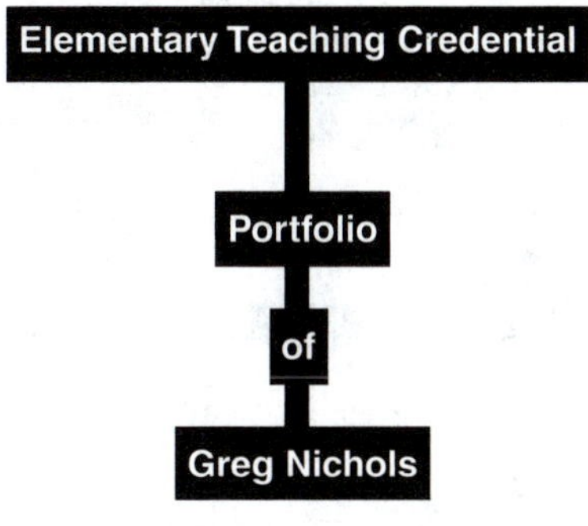

A. Highlighted text from opening page

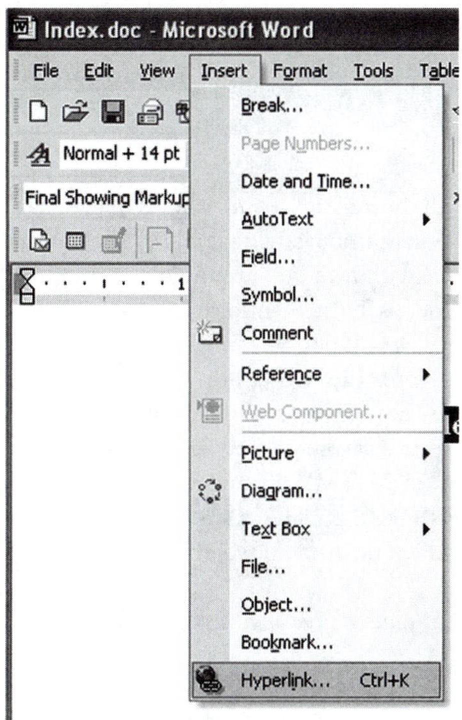

B. Inserting hyperlink

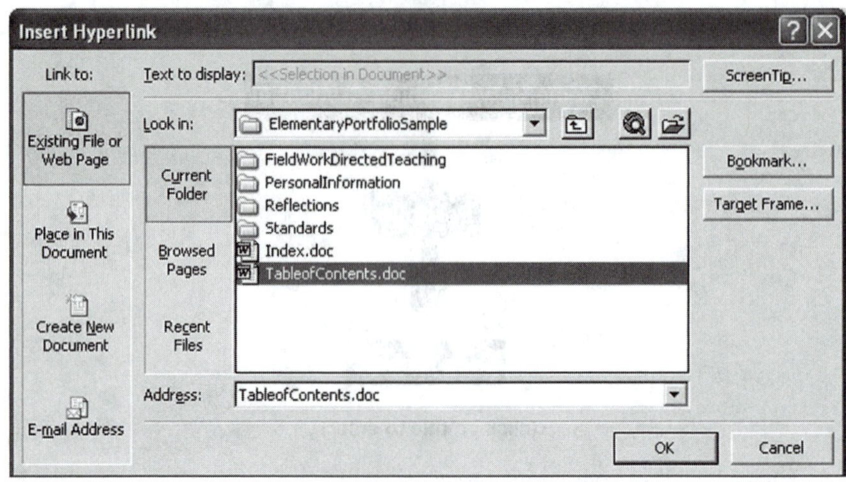

Figure 7.7 Insert Hyperlink Dialog Box Connecting Word Documents

7. Then click on the table of contents file.

8. Then click OK.

Similar steps will be taken to link the artifacts back to the table of contents. It is extremely important that all of the folders and files for the portfolio are located within the main portfolio folder. If they are not, then when the main folder is burned onto a CD or copied to another storage device, folders and files will not be copied.

As mentioned before, the procedure is virtually the same for creating a link in a Word HTML document. The only difference is that instead of selecting Index.doc as for the Word document link, you would choose Index.htm for the Word HTML document.

Figure 7.8 shows the Insert Hyperlink dialog box for the HTML documents. Notice that the only difference is the addition of HTM files and a few new folders.

So, to repeat, the steps in creating a hyperlink in Word are as follows:

1. Open the document in Word.

2. Highlight the words that will be the "clickable" text.

3. Click on Insert.

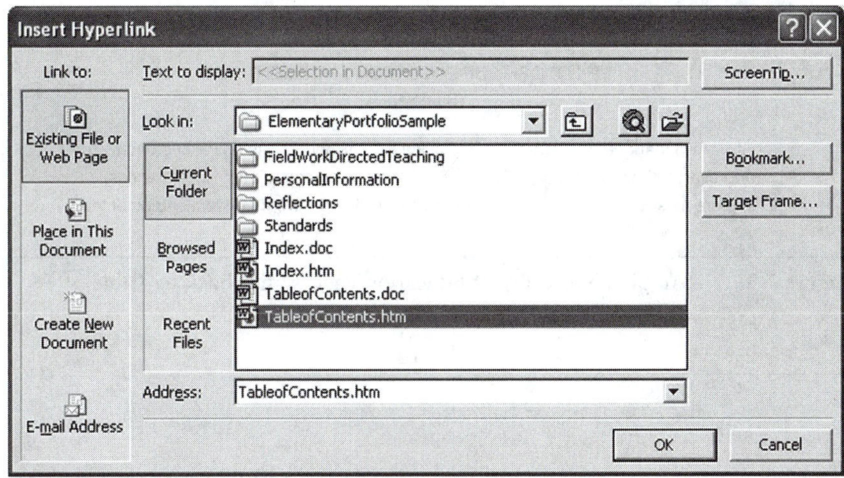

Figure 7.8 Insert Hyperlink Dialog Box Connecting HTML Documents

4. Hyperlink.
5. From the Insert Hyperlink dialog box, select the file to be linked.
6. Then click OK.

Linking With the Table of Contents

Now that the opening page is linked to the table of contents, it is time to link all the topics from the table of contents page to the supporting materials. This time, open the TableofContents file (Word file or Word HTML file). Follow the same steps described previously for each file. The same procedure for linking is followed no matter what kind of file is being linked. If the file to be linked to is not in the folder that is currently open, either double click on the folder to open it (if it is visible in the dialog box) or click the down arrow to the right of "Look in:" and navigate to the correct folder (Figures 7.7 and 7.8).

After all of the links are made from the table of contents page, half the work is done. Currently, users can travel from the table of contents to the linked pages but not back again. So by making minor modifications to each file, a link back to the table of contents will be added. At the top of the page (Figure 7.9), the bottom of the page, or both top and bottom, add a line of text that reads, "Back

Back to Table of Contents

PHILOSOPHY OF EDUCATION STATEMENT
(Sample)

I believe that one major factor in improving K-12 schools rests on valuing each and every child regardless of his or her individual background and circumstances. Educators must strive to be responsive to every child and have an understanding of the

Figure 7.9 Sample Philosophy of Education Page With "Back to Table of Contents" Link Added

to Table of Contents." Once this is added, then save the file. This added text will be used to create a link back to the TableofContents page.

Here are the steps to link this back to the table of contents:

1. Highlight the text that will be linked: "Back to Table of Contents."
2. Then click on Insert.
3. Then click on Hyperlink (Table 7.10B). The Insert Hyperlink dialog box will open (Figure 7.8). The Insert Hyperlink box opens to the folder where the file being worked on is saved. In most cases, this will not be the same folder as the table of contents file.
4. To navigate back to that file, click on the down arrow to the right of "Look in:" and choose the main portfolio folder. In this case, the folder would be ElementaryPortfolioSample. In this folder, the file TableofContents is found.
5. Click on the file TableofContents.
6. Then click OK.

Without these links back, the user will have difficulty returning to the table of contents and will need to restart the portfolio each time to be able to open any of the other artifacts. In some cases, along with the link to the table of contents, a second link may point to further supporting materials. This would be the case for the "mammals" lesson plan we mentioned before. On the lesson plan, links would be added to each of the four worksheets and to the PowerPoint presentation. Remember, if this is a Web-based portfolio, all of these files would be previously converted to htm files.

Save Your Changes

As modifications are completed (or are in progress), be sure to save the changes and save often. The modifications that need to be made are the creation of all the links on the table of contents page to the supporting documents and then a link back to the table of contents page on each of the supporting documents. In some cases, as in the mammals lesson plan, there may be an additional link to more supporting materials.

"Save files often" cannot be said often enough. In addition, save a copy in a different location (on another disk or computer). Then, at the end of your work session, consider making a copy of the entire portfolio folder. This copy should include some type of date indicator. For instance, if the original folder is named "elementaryportfolio," the backup could be named "elementaryportfolio_6-22." This would indicate that the version was saved on June 22. This aids in identifying the most recently revised version.

Test the Links

It is a good idea to test each link as it is created. Word allows a link to be followed by holding down the Control key (Ctrl) and then clicking on it. Word HTML files should also be tested, by using a Web browser. Notice that if there is no returning link on the other page, navigation is awkward. Once all of the links have been created, test the entire portfolio. It is easy to miss a link that returns to the table of contents or links to the wrong file. Should a link navigate to a wrong file, editing the link is simple:

1. Highlight the hyperlinked text.
2. Right click the highlighted text.
3. Select Insert Hyperlink. The Insert Hyperlink dialog box will open, as in Figures 7.7 and 7.8.
4. Select the correct file.
5. Click OK.

Once all the links are working, make sure all the files are saved, and then make a copy of the Portfolio folder. This copy should be burned onto a CD or copied to a large-capacity storage drive.

Creating an Electronic Portfolio Using PowerPoint

What are the differences between creating the electronic portfolio using Word and creating it using PowerPoint? The main difference is found in the opening file and the table of contents. These two files will be created in PowerPoint instead of Word. Just like in the electronic portfolio in Word, the artifacts have already been created. These artifacts are saved as various types of files (e.g., Word, PowerPoint, PDF, JPG). PowerPoint is used to connect all the files together for easy access.

PowerPoint is used for creating not only teacher education portfolios but also professional portfolios used in educational administration, educational counseling, and master's degrees.

In our scenario, Rachel, a secondary teaching credential candidate, was more familiar with PowerPoint and wanted to create her electronic portfolio with it. Here is how she would do it:

Organizing the files and folders is exactly the same as stated earlier in "Getting Started—Naming Files." Remember to use only one-word names or names that use an underscore (_) between the words instead of spaces. Start out by creating a main Portfolio folder. In this case, it will be called "SingleSubjectPortfolioSample." Inside this folder will be subfolders that correspond to the categories in the table of contents. Inside each of the subfolders will be all of the files that contain the artifacts (Table 7.7). In Table 7.11, A and B, the topics from the single subject table of contents are used to create corresponding subfolders. The artifacts supporting these topics will be contained inside these subfolders. The only files outside of the subfolders are the PowerPoint version of the opening file (Index.ppt) and the PowerPoint HTML version of the opening file (Index.htm).

Creating the Opening Page and Table of Contents in PowerPoint

PowerPoint offers a wide variety of backgrounds for designing an opening slide for your portfolio. Remember to choose a background that allows the text to be seen clearly and read easily. The font color may need to be changed so it will stand out for easy reading.

Once the background is chosen, choose a "Title slide" layout for the opening slide. This slide should contain your name, the purpose of the portfolio, and an appropriate graphic (Figure 7.10). PowerPoint doesn't provide as much height as Word does, so don't try to put too much information on

Table 7.11 Listing of Folders (A) and Files (B) for Single Subject Credential

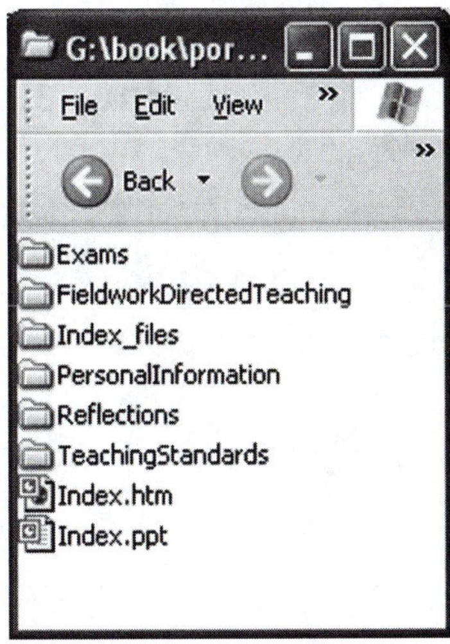

A. Listing of the folders and the opening file in the main portfolio folder

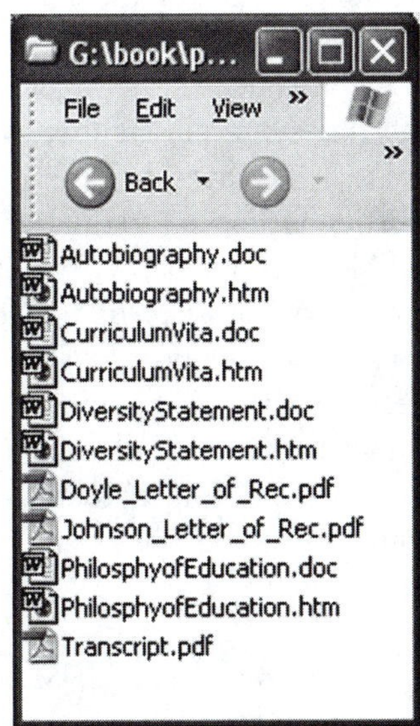

B. Listing of the Word documents and converted Word HTML documents contained in the PersonalInformation subfolder

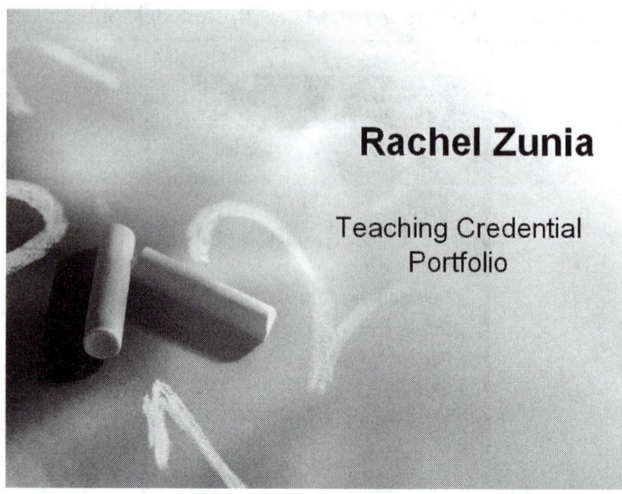

Figure 7.10 Portfolio Opening Page in PowerPoint

one slide. Click the New Slide icon or click on Insert, New Slide. The next slide will be the table of contents. Because there isn't a lot of room on each slide, the table of contents lists only the main categories. Each category will link to another slide that will list the subcategories, and these subcategories will be linked to the supporting artifacts. The first two slides for the table of contents are shown in Table 7.12. Once the table of contents is set, then it will be linked to its supporting artifacts. It would be a good idea to include one more slide after the table of contents. On this slide, one can thank the viewers for taking their time to consider your qualifications. It would be a nice way to let the viewer know the portfolio presentation is completed. Save the PowerPoint file, name the file "Index.ppt," and save it in the SingleSubjectPortfolioSample folder. This should be the only file in that folder. All the other files are contained in subfolders inside the folder named SingleSubjectPortfolioSample. In Word, the opening page and the table of contents are in two separate files. In PowerPoint, they are on different slides but in the same file.

Remember, if the portfolio is going to be HTML-based, don't create the links until all the artifacts have been converted to HTML (all except the PDFs and JPGs).

Again, one might ask, "PowerPoint or HTML, which one is right?" PowerPoint is a presentation tool, so viewing an electronic portfolio works well. Like Word, PowerPoint can be converted to HTML. The main thing is

Table 7.12 The First Two Slides From the Table of Contents in PowerPoint

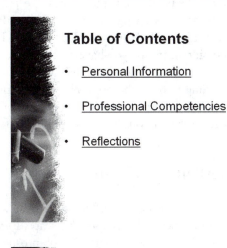

Table of Contents

- Personal Information
- Professional Competencies
- Reflections

Personal Information

- *Philosophy of Education*
- *Diversity Statement*
- *Autobiography*
- *Curriculum Vita*
- *Letters of Recommendation*
- *Transcripts*

to decide how the portfolio is to be viewed *before* linking all the files. If you decide to go with the HTML conversion, it is strongly suggested that you convert all Word and PowerPoint files to HTML instead of converting just the PowerPoint files. Another consideration is whether the person viewing the HTML version of the portfolio is using Netscape or Internet Explorer. There is one extra feature available in Explorer, which is a full-screen, Web-based slide show. If Word documents are not converted to HTML, when a Word document is accessed, Word opens and the documents are viewed in Word, not in a Web browser.

As in the previous discussion about Word or HTML, it all depends on how you would like to present the portfolio. Is the intent to keep it on CD or post it to the Web? Will the person viewing the portfolio need PowerPoint and Word on their computer or just a Web browser? Don't forget, just because you convert it to HTML doesn't mean that you have post it on the Web. It can still be distributed on CD, and it is easier to view in HTML.

If your portfolio is going to be Web-based (uploaded to the Web or not), continue with this section. If your portfolio is going to be PowerPoint-based, skip this section and go to the section on creating links.

Converting PowerPoint to HTML

Consider who will be looking at your PowerPoint file. What kind of computer will they have and what browser will they use—Netscape, Explorer, or something else? Don't narrow the viewing audience (or job prospects) by thinking that everyone uses Internet Explorer. Yes, PowerPoint converted to HTML does work *best* in Explorer, but that's because they are both Microsoft products. By making a minor setting adjustment, your presentation will be available to more than just Explorer users. In PowerPoint, follow these steps:

1. Click on Tools.
2. Then click on Options, and an options dialog box will open.
3. On the General tab, click on Web Options as shown in Figure 7.11. Click on the Browsers tab. Make sure that the option for "People who view this Web page will be using:" is changed to "Microsoft Internet Explorer 4, or Netscape Navigator 4, or later." This will enable more people to view your portfolio.
4. Another option that one might want (but which is not necessary) is "Save an additional version of the presentation for older browsers." Now most people have newer browsers, but remember that you are dealing with schools, and some schools may *not* have new browsers.

With that said, let's get on to converting these files.

1. Open your PowerPoint file that contains the opening slide and the table of contents.
2. Click on File.
3. Click on Save As Web Page. The Save As dialog box will open (Figure 7.12).

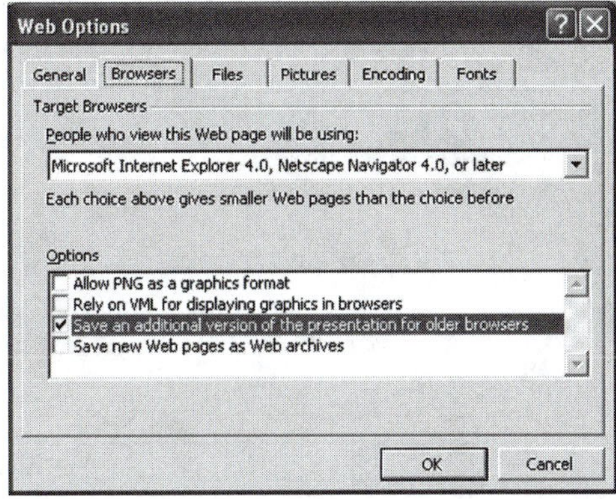

Figure 7.11 PowerPoint Web Options Dialog Box

4. As with Word, click on the Change Title button and add a short but descriptive title for the page. Remember, this is not the file name, just the name that appears at the top of the Web browser window. Make sure that the file will be saved in your main Portfolio folder (in this case, it is called SingleSubject PortfolioSample).

5. Then click Save.

PowerPoint will create an HTML file and a folder with all of the needed files. Don't erase this folder, or the presentation will not work! Follow these same steps and convert any other PowerPoint files included in the portfolio, making sure to save them in their original folders. When finished, convert all of the Word documents to HTML also. That way, when the portfolio is viewed, all the artifacts are viewed in the Web browser and Word doesn't need to be opened. Refer to these steps, which were covered earlier in this chapter.

Creating Links in PowerPoint

Creating links in PowerPoint is similar to Word. In PowerPoint, two types of links will be created. The first type of link connects within the PowerPoint file. The second type of link connects to other files (just like what was done previously in Word). This first example is linking within a PowerPoint file. With the opening file opened in PowerPoint, move to the first slide for the

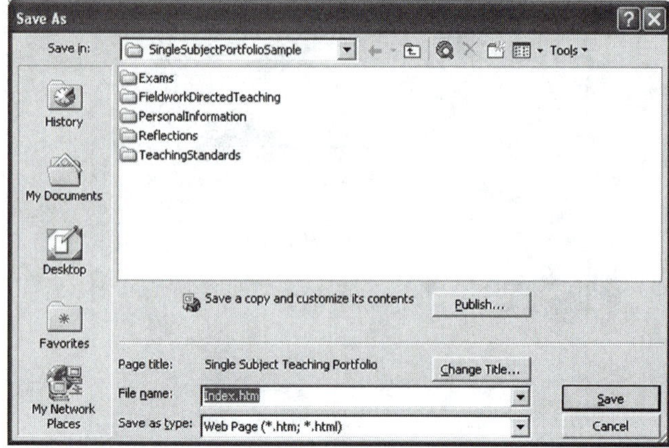

Figure 7.12 The PowerPoint Save As Web Page Dialog Box

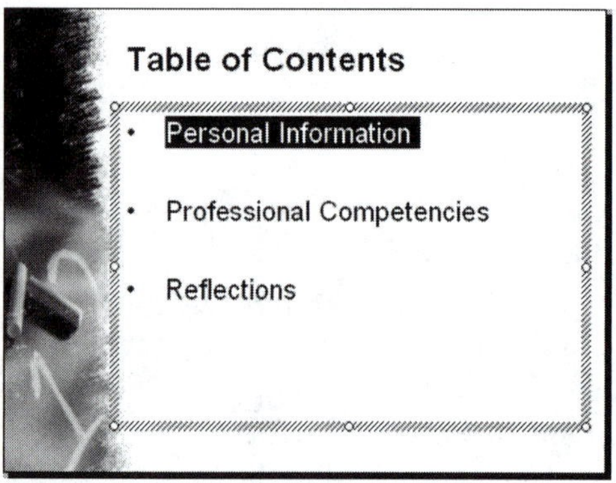

Figure 7.13 Highlighted Item to Be Linked

table of contents. Unlike in Word, the opening page and table of contents are already linked by the slide show. To create a link that connects within a PowerPoint file, do the following:

1. Highlight the first point (Figure 7.13).
2. Then click on Insert.

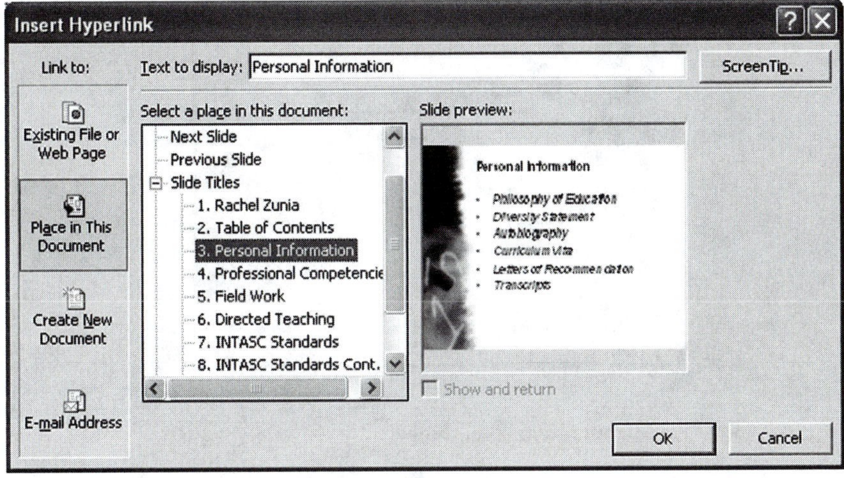

Figure 7.14 PowerPoint Insert Hyperlink Dialog Box

Click on the Place in This Document option, then on the slide to be linked to.

3. Then click Hyperlink, and the Insert Hyperlink dialog box will open just like it did in Word (Figure 7.14).
4. In the "Link to:" column, choose Place in This Document.
5. In the Select a Place in This Document column, choose the slide that corresponds to the highlighted text.
6. Click OK and the link is complete.

Now we will create the second type of link. This link connects to another file. To create a link to another file in PowerPoint, follow these steps:

1. Highlight the first point (Figure 7.15).
2. Then click on Insert.
3. Then click Hyperlink, and the Insert Hyperlink dialog box will open just like it did in Word (Figure 7.16).
4. In the "Link to:" column, choose Existing File of Web Page.
5. In the "Look In:" column, double click on the PersonalInformation folder, which is where the Philosophy of Education file can be found.

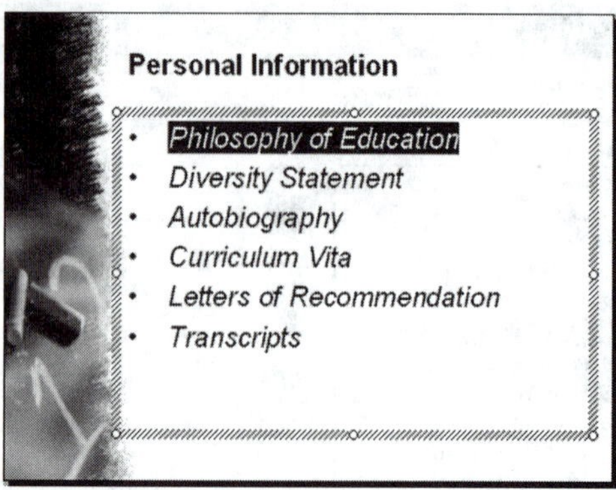

Figure 7.15 Highlighted Item to Be Linked

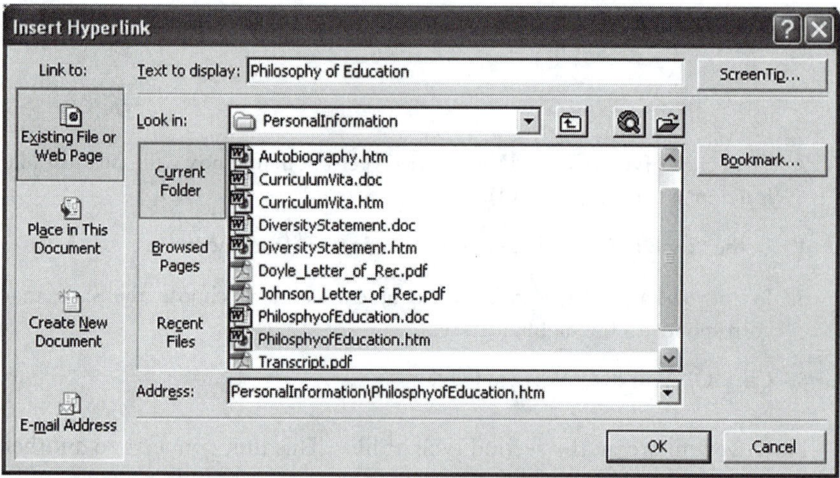

Figure 7.16 PowerPoint Insert Hyperlink Dialog Box

Click on the Existing File or Web Page option, then double click on the folder that houses the artifact to be linked to.

6. Then click on the file PhilosophyofEducation.htm or Philosphyof Education.doc if it is not Web-based.
7. Click OK and the link is complete.

If the folder that the supporting material is in is not visible, click on the down arrow to the right of "Look in:" and navigate to the folder where it is located. It is extremely important that all of the folders for the portfolio are located within the main portfolio folder. If they are not, when the main folder is burned onto a CD or copied to another storage device, all of the folders will not be copied. These same steps will be repeated to link all of the artifacts to the table of contents.

As mentioned before, save the files and save them often. After all your links are created, test them. Additional links may be needed to link multiple file examples together, as mentioned previously with the mammals lesson plan. Unlike Word, PowerPoint automatically opens a new window for each link, so links back to the table of contents are not needed. To return to the table of contents, just close the window. After all the links are working, save the portfolio and create a backup of the entire project. It can now be burned to a CD or uploaded to a Web site.

If any additional materials need to be added in the future, add new folders, files, and links as necessary. Save the changes, test the links, and the portfolio is ready to be distributed again.

Summary

Whether the portfolio is created in Word or PowerPoint, the real work is in collecting and organizing the files. All files must be contained within a portfolio folder, then organized inside this portfolio folder using subfolders. With this file structure in place, updating or editing the portfolio will be fairly easy. In addition, by keeping all the files inside the portfolio folder, it is easy to create multiple copies of the portfolio.

Electronic portfolios are versatile, living documents. As candidates progress in their careers, artifacts can easily be added. This progression may even result in a change in focus for the portfolio. This change can be reflected by updating the opening page and table of contents to fit the new focus.

Useful Resources

Adobe (Acrobat PDF writer; Premiere digital video editing software; Photoshop graphics package)—www.adobe.com

CutePDF Writer—www.cutepdf.com

FolioLive portfolios—www.foliolive.com
International Society of Technology in Education (ISTE) and National Education Technology Standards—www.iste.org
Online tutorials—www.atomiclearning.com
Online tutorials—www.lynda.com
Pinnacle Software (digital video software and hardware)—www.pinnaclesys.com
Scanning tips—www.scantips.com
TaskStream portfolios—www.taskstream.com

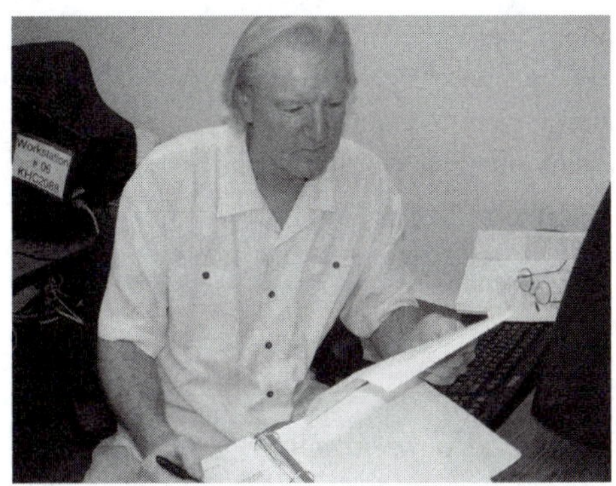

8

After the Credential Program, Now What?

Keeping the Portfolio Alive

A professional portfolio can help. It can be a tool that enables you to make sense out of a myriad of experiences. It also can bring into focus a clear picture of yourself as a growing, changing professional. Equally as significant, it can be a convincing, effective vehicle for you to demonstrate to others in a meaningful way the skills and knowledge you have gained in something as complex as teaching.

—Campbell, Cignetti, Melenyzer, Nettles, & Wyman (2001), *How to Develop a Professional Portfolio: A Manual for Teachers*

Chapter Objectives

The reader will be able to

- describe the value of continuous portfolio development,
- describe ways to use the portfolio as an instrument for reflection and self-evaluation,

- retool the portfolio for academic and career advancement,
- use the portfolio in interviews and other settings to present evidence of academic and professional growth and achievement.

Scenario

Linda and Glenn had successfully completed their degree and credential programs. Glenn decided that he wanted to start teaching as soon as he could find a position. He wanted to teach in the neighborhood where he grew up. Linda was thinking about substituting while she decided whether she really wanted a teaching career. Although she had passed all of her courses, her student teaching experience was rated only as "meets standards." She also was thinking about applying to graduate school. She thought she might need a master's degree to deepen her knowledge about teaching, particularly teaching reading to children whose primary language is not English.

Glenn told Linda that he had talked with some friends who had been teaching for a while and they had shared information about applying for jobs. One friend, Miguel, had updated and used his portfolio in several interviews. He mentioned that reviewing his artifacts and presenting some information from his portfolio gave him a sense of security and confidence. The more he used it, the more at ease he became with the process. He had to do some minor revisions after the first interview. He received many positive responses about his portfolio documents. Miguel had several job offers. He wasn't sure if the portfolio had been the pivotal factor in securing a job, but he felt that it gave him confidence in presenting himself.

Another friend, Rick, told Glenn that he also had used his portfolio in an interview, but it turned out to be a disaster. He brought his three-inch hardcover binder to the interview. This was the same one he had from his teacher preparation program. When he opened the binder to find some information, his notebook fell off the table and the papers scattered all over the floor. He was so flustered and embarrassed that he was barely able to answer subsequent questions. Rick eventually found a job, but it was not the top one that he was seeking. He wondered if better preparation and use of the portfolio could have helped him secure the job he really wanted.

The following week, Linda and Glenn talked at graduation rehearsal. Glenn told Linda that he had several interviews coming up. He had visited the career office, and they had given him some ideas about how to prepare for interviews. However, he was feeling insecure about the interviews and was curious about how his portfolio might help in an interview setting. Linda suggested that he ask his friend Miguel to give him some tips and to help him with a mock interview. Linda volunteered to participate in the mock interview. She wondered if the portfolio would be useful in making her competitive for a master's program. As they continued to talk, they concluded that having information about the use of the portfolio in interviews and other career advancement experiences might have been a valuable enhancement to their teacher preparation program.

Overview

In reflecting on experiences and research about portfolio development, one can conclude that the reflection and self-evaluation phase that the learner engages in while assembling and organizing the portfolio has value for life-long learning. Development of portfolios should not be terminated at program or degree completion. Portfolios have the potential to become meaningful enhancements for job searches and interviews, job evaluations, and most important, as dynamic documents for self-evaluation and accomplishments in one's career. Examining one's portfolio can be a source of pride in what has been achieved and an inspiration for further accomplishments.

This chapter offers some suggestions on how to continue the portfolio experience throughout teaching or other professional careers, including some ways to retool the portfolio for specific purposes and presentations.

The Portfolio as a Reflective Companion

As the candidates transition from preparation programs to their next phase of professional development, the portfolio can become an interactive, reflective companion for documenting growth and development. The reflection, inquiry, and evaluation skills that were acquired during preparation programs are resources and support for future professional growth. Preservice professionals, who have become experienced in presenting their portfolios, now have some facility in how to articulate, highlight, and document their very best achievements. This is a significant professional asset.

What might be some future uses for a portfolio during your professional career? There are several academic and professional areas in which the portfolio has constant utility. Up-to-date, well-developed portfolios have many potential benefits. Table 8.1 suggests some possible arenas for future portfolio use.

In the next section we suggest some ways to retool the portfolio for different purposes.

Table 8.1 Academic and Career-Advancement Uses of Portfolios

Academic	*Use*
Graduate School/Credential Programs	Interview preparation: Provides a readily available review of professional achievements, strengths, and weaknesses prior to the interview; can be used for mock interviews. In the interview: Demonstrates the candidate's ability to document and provide evidence of achievements in a professional arena; provides readily available past academic records and selected graded course papers that are related to the academic area in which the candidate is seeking admission.
Professional Areas	*Use*
Self-Evaluation	Provides a powerful internal source for pride and joy in accomplishments, as well as information on how one needs to grow professionally. With self-evaluation, the portfolio uses continuous reflection to self-assess progress, what is working, and what needs to change in knowledge, skills, and/or disposition. One can seek out critical friends, define professional development needs, and take pride in what is accomplished. The portfolio Artifacts Organizer provides quick overviews regarding professional levels and focus. Self-evaluation has the potential to inform supervisor evaluation.
Future Employment/ Job Interviews	Assessment: Assists in assessing whether knowledge, skills, and dispositions are aligned with employment opportunities. Interview preparation: Provides a readily available review of professional achievements, strengths, and weaknesses prior to the interview; can be used for mock interviews. In the interview: Has the potential to provide focused evidence of accomplishments in areas related to school/district goals; demonstrates the candidate's ability to document and provide evidence of achievements in professional arenas; if needed, academic achievements can also be showcased.

Academic	*Use*
Promotional/ Lateral/Advanced Certification Opportunities	Gives candidates a competitive edge, providing they are able to show quality artifacts in the areas that are being sought for the position/certificate. If the portfolio is kept up-to-date, it will facilitate the gathering of materials that will be needed, such as developing a portfolio for National Board Certification.
Supervisor Evaluation	Provides documentation for what has been accomplished and should demonstrate the levels of accomplishment; provides evidence of program, project implementation; may provide for nontraditional types of information, such as parent, student, and colleague letters; electronic information.
Professional Resource Bank	Can demonstrate professional efficacy and is a ready source of guidelines for future projects; a rich source for literature and documentation of successful achievements or examples of how challenges need to be addressed; provides a resource for sharing information with colleagues.
Professional Development	Identifies the areas where professional development needs to begin, deepen, and/or be revisited from another perspective. One can self-identify patterns of strengths and where improvement is needed.

Retooling the Portfolio

Future uses of the portfolio require retooling to accommodate specific uses, such as job interviews. A *comprehensive portfolio* or working portfolio (see Chapter 1) can be developed and kept in a file drawer, box, binder, or electronic format. The comprehensive portfolio is an up-to-date storehouse from which artifacts and other materials are selected for a variety of professional purposes. The contents are concrete evidence of professional accomplishments that are collected over time and are similar to those described in Chapter 5. As one develops and improves professional competencies, new and improved documentation should replace earlier items. The comprehensive portfolio will have more information than is needed for any one type of portfolio described in Table 8.1. This portfolio storage system still needs to have a current table of contents and some type of Artifacts Organizer for ease of locating and analyzing artifacts as they relate to goals, areas, and standards.

In retooling the portfolio for specific purposes, it is critical for candidates to do their homework. Employers like to feel that a prospective candidate has a special desire to work for them and is one who has some familiarity with their setting. If candidates do not do their homework, they may leave the impression that they are not focused on a specific job or goal or have no particular interest in the school or district. When schools or districts are selective about whom to employ, those who do not research current employment opportunities may end up at the bottom of the opportunity list or the candidate may accept a position that is not well suited for his or her talents and interests.

Researching areas related to one's goals also applies to academic advancement. Before applying to a college or university, you should research programs, types of degrees, professors' research and publications foci, and the vision, philosophy, and the institution's mission. Also, inquire about job placement records and support for career and academic advancement. Web sites provide valuable, current information about enrollment, demographics, achievement, goals, organization, and so on. Site visits can provide copies of newsletters and other information about institutional climate, setting, and conditions. For school or district employment searches, it is advisable to tour the area of prospective employment to become familiar with students' neighborhoods. This will give information not only about neighborhoods but also about business, community, recreational, and religious sites in the area.

It is advisable to secure and seek out background information about desired career-advancement opportunities. For lateral or promotional opportunities, potential candidates need to get as familiar as possible with the job requirements, time demands, role expectations, salary ranges, education requirements, and other unique aspects of the position. Talking with others who hold similar positions may be useful, but a note of caution is in order. Personal experiences and perspectives vary and have the potential to inaccurately sway a candidate's view of a prospective job opportunity.

Once the research has occurred, it is time to retool and tailor the comprehensive portfolio to align it as tightly as possible to its specific use. Most future uses of the portfolio will include many of the contents listed in Chapter 5. The major areas include personal information and documentation of achievement in professional standards. The resume, references, and professional evaluations begin to play a more prominent role in academic and career advancement, and in promotions and lateral position changes. Accomplishments, talents, and personal characteristics as viewed by others will be noted by those seeking to hire or grant admission to candidates.

What Patterns of Strengths or Gaps Exist?

The Artifacts Organizer and Table of Contents (see Chapter 5) can assist with analyzing how much documentation is available in the areas of focus for a job or for seeking higher-education admission. After the initial review of artifacts, you may note patterns and gaps in experiences or knowledge, or both. Analyze which areas appear to be strengths, those needing development, and those areas in which there is minimal or no experience. If there are major disconnects between jobs or other requirements, candidates may need to reconsider whether this is the optimum time to seek advancement opportunities.

On the other hand, evidence may exist of achievements that have not become a part of the portfolio. These artifacts should be collected at this time. If weak areas can be addressed at some level, they should be. If there are gaps in knowledge or experience but a candidate wants to move forward, it would be wise to determine how those areas will be developed. Many interviewers do ask candidates to identify their strengths and weaknesses and to describe how they plan to improve in weak areas.

Table 8.2 gives an example of a way to document areas of strength and those that need development. The table or some other organizational tool helps to facilitate the analysis and can be used to prepare for advancement opportunities and for self- and supervisor evaluation. Consider this a tool that should be updated at least on an annual basis. This provides an excellent opportunity for self-evaluation. A template is provided on the CD.

Selecting Contents for the Portfolio

After candidates have done their research and analyzed patterns of strengths, weaknesses, and gaps, it is time to assemble a focused portfolio for a given purpose. Table 8.1 shows some examples of several different types of portfolios and their possible uses. The major areas include personal information and documentation of achievement in professional standards.

Review Chapter 2, Table 2.3, on the action research process involved in the selection of artifacts, as well as the section in Chapter 3 on how to transform artifacts into evidence, including Tables 3.2 and 3.5. This information proves valuable in the evaluation and selection of artifacts for inclusion. The

Table 8.2 Gap Analysis Tool—Profile of Strengths and Areas for Development

Date: **Current Position:**

Focus Area (Goal, Standard, etc.)	*Areas of Strength*	*Areas That Need Development*	*Strategies to Improve*
Example: INTASC Principle 1, Knowledge of Subject Matter	**Knowledge**—3.8 GPA, all A's in my major (mathematics); current in my subject matter; member of National Council of Teacher of Mathematics (NCTM); attended several mathematics conferences; currently enrolled in a master's degree program.	**Skills**—Still learning to differentiate instruction; not much documentation to demonstrate success in this area. **Dispositions**—Not sure that I have high expectations for kids that are not achieving; not sure I believe they can achieve in my Algebra 1 classes or at higher math levels.	**Skills**—Currently working with a mathematics coach; I am observing her teach, and she is observing my classes and critiquing my lessons and then coming in for a follow-up; this will continue. **Dispositions**—I need to find out about places where kids are succeeding in math and see what those teachers do; I need to believe that it can happen; I plan to seek help in this area by observing others and learning to use their strategies; I am reading some research, discussing my problem with my instructors at the college, and looking at Web sites for information.
Continue with other focus, goal, or standards areas			

My Reflection: Write a reflective statement about strengths and weaknesses. This will be good preparation for the interview.

focused portfolio might begin with three major components: current personal information, achievement in professional standards, and letters of reference. As previously mentioned, at a minimum, update material on an annual basis and place update reminders on a calendar. Resumes and other pertinent information should be kept updated electronically.

These *focus portfolios* are prepared for a specific purpose and with a goal in mind, such as employment or promotion. They differ in size, function, and portability from a comprehensive portfolio. Table 8.3 gives an example of how to organize artifacts to prepare concurrently for various focused portfolios. This requires a retooling of the Artifacts Organizer presented in Chapter 5. The organizer in Table 8.3 can be used as an indicator system for briefly noting *yes, no,* or *maybe* about inclusion of an artifact, or it can be expanded to include descriptive and reflective notations. The notations will probably prove more valuable but will require a time commitment. Opportunities sometimes become available unexpectedly, and an updated information resource provides an up-to-the-minute labor-saving tool.

The sample artifacts in Table 8.3 have notations and indications of whether they should be considered for review or for inclusion in a focus portfolio, or both. There are examples of indicators for inclusion (*yes, maybe, no*) and some examples of notations. This organizer is designed as an initial system only for selecting artifacts for use in focus areas. Requirements for some portfolios, such as National Board Certification and other specific areas, involve more extensive preparation. A template for Table 8.3 is included in the CD.

Once the documents for the focused portfolio have been finalized, create a table of contents for each focus area. This serves as a preparation tool and as a document that can be shared with others. Campbell et al. (2001) show a way to display contents using an organizational tool titled "Portfolio at a Glance." This tool gives a thumbnail overview by naming the artifacts under each category that are included in the portfolio. A modified table of contents could serve a similar purpose.

Previous supervisor evaluations, memos of corrective actions, or other documents that contain information with commendations and recommendations for development should be reviewed for inclusion.

Portfolio Presentation for Career and Educational Advancement

Many candidates who used portfolios for employment interviews share their sense of confidence about the abilities it describes. They also articulate their

Table 8.3 Artifacts Organizer for Academic and Career-Advancement-Focused Portfolios (Sample)

Review and/or Inclusion in Focus Portfolio: Yes No Maybe

Artifact	*Professional Standard, Goal, Academic Area*	*Focus: Master's Degree Program*	*Focus: Curriculum Coach*	*Focus: National Board Certification*
Case Studies Dates: 1/05; 6/05	INTASC Principle 1—Knowledge of Subject Matter; Knowledge of Human Development and Learning; Adapting Instruction for Individual Learning	Yes—Able to apply knowledge to classroom teaching; demonstrates academic writing and beginning skills as a researcher.	Yes—Demonstrates curriculum knowledge; collaboration with peers; leadership in my department; ability to self-evaluate and critique my teaching.	Yes—Case study links to National Board for Professional Teaching Standards for Mathematics: Adolescence and Young Adulthood Certificate. Good example of description, analysis, and reflection (still needs work).
Agendas and students' work and achievement data from Lesson Study Groups Dates: September 2003–June 2005, approximately every three weeks	INTASC Principle 1—Knowledge of Subject Matter; Adapting Instruction for Individual Learning; Multiple Instructional Strategies; Assessment of Student Learning	Yes—Recent comments from my colleagues indicate that my plans, student work, and assessments demonstrate outstanding knowledge of assessment in the area of content	Yes—Recently (see agendas), I have facilitated lesson sessions; my facilitation, leadership, and communication skills with colleagues are becoming very effective; we have	Yes—Most recent artifacts are aligned with all Five Core Propositions: (1) Teachers are committed to students and their learning; (2) Teachers know the subjects they teach and how

Artifact	*Professional Standard, Goal, Academic Area*	*Focus: Master's Degree Program*	*Focus: Curriculum Coach*	*Focus: National Board Certification*
		standards and my achievement data indicate effective teaching.	professional dialogues about improvement, challenge assumptions about what is possible, and leave with improvement strategies; a sense of efficacy pervades our group.	to teach those subjects to students (3) Teachers are responsible for managing and monitoring student learning; (4) Teachers think systematically about their practice and learn from experience; (5) Teachers are members of learning communities.
Teaching Video Date: October 2004; January 2005; May 2005	Nos. 1–8	**Maybe**	**Maybe**	**Yes**

accomplishments prior to and during the interview. Possessing real-world, concrete evidence to demonstrate achievements helps in responding to interview questions. Candidates also share that some potential employers are favorably impressed with the assembled body of information about their achievements. However, there can be challenges in using portfolios in an interview. Remember Rick's experience, described in the opening scenario.

His portfolio fell off the table and scattered all over. He had not retooled or updated his portfolio.

To prepare to use the portfolio in an interview setting for career or academic advancements, candidates need to follow these steps:

1. Select contents. In prior sections, we discussed retooling, analyzing strengths and weakness, and organizing artifacts by focus areas. Now it is time to select the *key contents for the focused portfolio*. These are the best of the best. We recommend including about two artifacts for each goal, standard, or job area. The resume should be added, and, if critical to the interview, so should other pertinent personal information documents.

2. Select container. Next, select and prepare the container for the portfolio contents. Review Chapter 6 for detailed suggestions on highlighting information, for example. A container should have a professional appearance and allow ease in accessing the documents, so that no attention will be diverted from the interviewee. For hard-cover portfolios, a binder with a zipper gives a professional appearance. For organizing the contents, tabs, sticky notes, and other tools can be used for quick location of documents. A soft-cover binder that can be inserted in a briefcase might also be used. If disks, CDs, or other electronic information is included, be sure to store them in pockets with three-hole plastic inserts or in the pocket of the notebook cover. Use three-hole plastic sheet protectors for ease of access and to protect documents. Another container that might be considered is a light plastic organizer with several pockets that can be labeled. These allow for folders to be inserted. Folders can be color coded and labeled. These organizers look attractive and professional. Attractive containers are constantly becoming available. Check with one of the many office supplies stores. All documents should be printed and photocopied on high-quality paper. Remember to bring only copies, not original documents, to leave with prospective employers. Electronic portfolios should be considered only if the interviewer(s) deem them appropriate. If so, candidates should check to see if the setting is appropriate and bring their own hardware. It is advisable to have hard-cover backups, or candidates can simply share a table of contents and/or provide a CD or Web site address—before, during, or after the interview.

3. Reviewer(s). Seek out someone who is a knowledgeable professional in the focus area of interest to review and give honest critiques about the authenticity, quality, and suitability of the contents, the organization for ease of presentation, and the appearance of the portfolio. Any documents that are

not adequate need to be deleted, unless they can be authentically retooled. Documents may need to be reformatted or have more substantive reflections. Another document from the comprehensive portfolio might be better suited, or the candidate may need to eliminate evidence in that area at this point. This may be an area for growth. Documents should not be redone or added to in ways that present inflated information. Only what is authentic should be included. Be sure to demonstrate appreciation of the review of your portfolio with a thank-you note or other gesture.

4. Mock interviews. Now it is time to rehearse how to use the portfolio in the interview. Be sure to do the research about the focus area discussed earlier in this chapter. Develop interview questions from the information gathered from the research. Setting up mock interviews gives candidates a chance to find out how well the container and organization of the portfolio work. Finding, taking out, pointing to, and presenting evidence for sharing in an interview requires lots of practice. In video- and audiotape rehearsals, be sure to rehearse potential interview questions with colleagues and friends. To get an honest assessment, give them a rating sheet. Always show appreciation with a thank-you note or other gesture. The previous suggestions may sound time-consuming, but consider the time spent as an investment in one's growth in becoming an outstanding reflective practitioner, who is able to self-evaluate one's professional growth and its potential value for career advancement.

5. Sharing the portfolio. It is probably advisable to inquire about sharing the portfolio prior to, during, or after the interview. If the portfolio is left, leave only a copy. Purchase an inexpensive but attractive soft-cover binder or something similar. Be sure it is labeled. Do not leave any confidential information, such as documents that may have a Social Security number or other personal information. Remember that the portfolio used during the interview is a supplement. Its purpose is to enhance, not to draw attention away from, the interviewee's comments or responses to questions. When the opportunity arises to refer to documentation in your portfolio, prepare the interviewers for the presentation of evidence from the portfolio with a statement such as, "I have had experience in this area, and I have a document in my portfolio that provides good illustrations of what I have accomplished." Quickly identify the document, hold on to it, and point to pertinent highlighted information as you answer the question. Do not pass the document around, because the interviewers may focus on the document and not fully listen to your answer. Share with them that you will leave this or any other appropriate information for their review.

There will be many opportunities during one's career to present portfolio documents for sharing. They will be valuable during evaluation conferences, with colleagues who are problem solving about a particular educational issue, during professional-development sessions, and in other professional and academic arenas. As the portfolio gets used and valued as a professional growth companion, it promises to become an essential professional-development tool for reflective educators.

Summary

This chapter discussed the portfolio as a continuous companion for professional development and its use in several areas of career and academic advancement. Maintaining a *comprehensive portfolio,* which is a storehouse covering a broad range of documents, gives evidence of professional accomplishments. This storehouse becomes the source for developing a *focused portfolio* that is assembled for specific academic or career-advancement purposes. Suggestions and templates were provided to assist in retooling the portfolio for specific goals, such as employment, professional advancement, and evaluation. Information was provided on how to use the portfolio to present evidence of professional growth and achievement for evaluations, interviews, and other career-development settings.

Research on professional practices indicates the increasing use of portfolios in colleges and schools of education, and in organizations, such as the National Board for Professional Standards, that require submissions of portfolios for documenting professional achievements. Schools and districts are urged to build on these practices—only after they have been assessed for authenticity, quality, and practicality of implementation. Implementing policies and designing ways for this to happen are challenges that require collaboration of professionals who are informed about and have the skills to implement the very best practices.

Useful Resources

Visit career-development offices, libraries, and Web sites that have useful information on preparing resumes and job-seeking-skill development.

For Further Reading

Brown, G., & Irby, B. J. (2000). *The career advancement portfolio* (2nd ed.). Thousand Oaks, CA: Corwin.

Campbell, D. M., Cignetti, P. B., Melenyzer, B. J., Nettles, D. H., & Wyman, R. M. W., Jr. (2001). *How to develop a professional portfolio: A manual for teachers* (2nd ed.). Boston: Allyn & Bacon.

The National Board for Professional Teaching Standards Web site, http://www.nbpts.org

Rieman, P. (2000). *Teaching portfolios: Presenting your professional best.* Boston: McGraw-Hill.

Satterthwaite, F., & D'Orsi, G. (2003). *The career portfolio workbook: Using the newest tool in your job-hunting arsenal to impress employers and land a great job.* New York: McGraw-Hill.

Portfolio Glossary of Terms

action research: a systematic approach used to improve one's own practice (Reason & Bradbury, 2004); a systematic execution or carefully articulated process of inquiry or questioning (Stringer, 2004). Psychologist Kurt Lewin is cited as the originator of action research. His goal was to promote social action through democratic decision making and active participation of practitioners in the research process (Holly, Arhar, & Kasten, 2005).

Adobe Acrobat writer: software created by Adobe Systems (www.adobe.com) that converts files into Portable Document Format (PDF).

application: demonstrates understanding of the subject by using knowledge in situations. It can be either expressive or inventive in nature (PATT, 2000).

artifacts: concrete examples of a person's work that are collected to demonstrate a particular knowledge, skill, or disposition (Brown & Irby, 2001).

assessment: the act or process of gathering data to better understand the strengths and weaknesses of student learning, as by observation, testing, interviews, and so forth (*The Literacy Dictionary*) (PATT, 2000). Assessment is an ongoing, developmental process to measure growth and change over time.

authentic: genuine, real-world, meaningful applications or examples. The use of actual products that are related to whatever is being observed or measured.

authentic assessment: any performance assessment that is a real-world, valid indicator of what is being measured. For example, real-world evidence of instructional practice may include requiring a candidate to write and implement a lesson in an actual classroom.

benchmark: the level of performance that is to be achieved at certain points. Note: Benchmarks serve as guideposts toward goals, objectives, and/or standards (CRESST). Descriptions of student performance at various developmental levels that contribute to the achievement of performance standards (*LEP Mathematics Assessment Training Indicators Manual*) (PATT, 2000).

burn: the act of recording information onto a CD or a DVD.

case study: a description and examination of a student, school, or district. The student, school, or district is usually kept anonymous.

CD: a compact disk; an optical medium that stores up to 700 megabytes per disk. Used mainly for music or file storage.

classroom management plan: an assignment in which teacher credential candidates begin developing a management system that works for them. It often includes a philosophical statement or theoretical foundation, a description of classroom rules, expectations and boundaries, a description of instructional and assessment strategies, and a process for motivating students to do their best (Charles, 2005).

commercial Web site: a Web site that is owned and operated by a person or business and is primarily used for commerce. There is generally a fee to use this kind of Web site.

competencies: abilities or proficiencies, what one is capable of doing; having requisite or adequate ability or qualities; having the capacity to function or develop in a particular way (*Merriam-Webster* Online).

content standard: articulates what students should understand and be able to do within specific content areas (e.g., identifies and uses appropriate strategies for various problem types).

criteria: guidelines, rules, characteristics, or dimensions that are used to judge the quality of student performance. Criteria indicate what we value in student responses, products, or performances. They may be holistic, analytic, general, or specific. Scoring rubrics are based on criteria and define what the criteria mean and how they are used (CRESST) (PATT, 2000).

culturally responsive: a practice and pedagogy that expects high student and educator achievement; one that is aligned and consistent with the cultural traditions and knowledge of students and draws upon, affirms, and validates prior experiences, language, frame of references, and performance styles of bicultural peoples (Johnson & Bush, 2005). Culturally responsive is sometimes referred to as "culturally relevant," "congruent," and "synchronized teaching" (Gay, 2000).

demographics: a statistical description of the composition of populations using indicators such as race, ethnicity, gender, language, and social economic status.

digital video: full-motion video stored in the form of 0s and 1s using the binary system. The video is either recorded on a digital camera or converted from analog video using a digital camera or computer with an analog-to-digital video capture card.

dispositions: attitudes, beliefs, or values. Dispositions are often viewed as the beliefs or affective and philosophical aspects of an individual.

DVD: a digital video disk; an optical media that stores up to 4.7 gigabytes per disk. Used mainly for video storage but can also hold files.

educational Web site: a Web site that is used primarily for education. Some of these sites are free, and others are fee-based.

electronic portfolio: a collection of artifacts housed digitally that are then organized and used for a variety of purposes, such as assessment, evaluation, and academic and professional advancement. These portfolios can be housed online or on a storage device.

evaluation: a final or summative process of determining overall progress. It is usually considered the culmination of a program or course of study.

final grade: the summative grade a person receives at the end of a course.

flash drives: large-capacity storage devices that use flash memory and a Universal Serial Bus (USB) connection. These range in size from 8 megabytes to 2 gigabytes. They are also sometimes called USB sticks, pen drives, or thumb drives.

formative: a developmental process that takes place over a period of time. Each part of the process builds on earlier stages. In formative evaluation, evidence is gathered at different times in a program or course to measure progress and to indicate areas of strength and those that need improvement. This evidence is used to form judgments on how to proceed, which are usually administered at the beginning and midpoints of, or at intervals during, a program.

gigabyte: about 1 billion bytes or 1,000 megabytes. It is abbreviated as GB.

high-stakes tests: tests that are used for accountability purposes to judge the relative goodness or weakness of institutions. These tests have high visibility and results for schools and districts and are usually published in newspapers and on state and district Web sites. For individuals, tests such as the SAT, ACT, and GRE are often used as part of the information to decide admission into programs, colleges, and so forth. Exit exams, such as high school exit exams, may determine whether an individual graduates from high school regardless of grades received.

HTML: hypertext markup language is the language used to create Web pages.

hyperlink: text or an object that, when clicked, jumps to the corresponding information.

inquiry: question(s) posed for investigation about practice. For portfolio purposes, inquiries involve a process of collecting, sorting, selecting, describing, analyzing, and evaluating evidence to answer questions on how well the evidence represents the candidate's accomplishment of a goal, standard, or objective.

INTASC Standards: the Interstate New Teacher Assessment and Support Consortium (INTASC) is a consortium of more than thirty states operating under the Council of Chief State School Officers (CCSSO), which has developed standards and an assessment process for initial teacher certification (Campbell, Melenyzer, Nettles, & Wyman, 2000).

JPG or **JPEG:** the Joint Photographic Experts Group is a compression format for color bitmapped images (photographs) and is named after the committee that set the compression standard. Files stored in this format have the .jpeg or .jpg extension.

link: *see* hyperlink.

live on the Web: information posted live is accessible to anyone.

mastery: the highest level of competency or proficiency in knowledge or skills.

medium/media: a specific kind of artistic technique or means of expression as determined by materials used or creative methods involved (e.g., writing or drawing).

megabyte: also called *meg* or *MB,* is about 1 million bytes.

NETS: National Educational Technology Standards (www.iste.org).

password protected: for security purposes, access to the information is available only with the correct password.

PDF: a Portable Document Format allows documents to be copied or e-mailed, and it doesn't matter what program was used originally to create the file. For example, if a friend sends a copy of an Inspiration software file and you do not have the program Inspiration, the file typically cannot be viewed. But if the file is converted to PDF, the file can be viewed as if it were photocopied and then attached to the e-mail. PDF files are viewed using Adobe Acrobat Reader (www.adobe .com), which is free software.

pen drives: *see* flash drives.

performance assessment: tasks that ask students to perform, create, or do something as a demonstration of what they know and can do; such tasks preferably require analytical thinking and problem-solving skills and often require trained human judgment for scoring (CTB/McGraw Hill, 1973) (PATT, 2000).

portable mass storage device: allows storage of large files (i.e., Zip drive, flash drive, USB mini hard drive).

portfolio: electronic or hard-copy documents that contain artifacts that have been selected over time to provide evidence of a learner's competency toward achieving a goal, standard, or objective. The artifacts provide evidence of knowledge, skills, and/or dispositions related to the standards, goals, or objectives. Portfolios can serve a variety of purposes. They may be used as assessment instruments, to display outstanding work, and to measure levels of competency for certification, graduation requirements, and career advancement.

portfolio presentation: the presentation of the portfolio to an audience as evidence of progress toward or completion of a standard, skill, knowledge, and so forth. This can be done during the program as a formative assessment, or at the end of a program as a summative evaluation. It can also be used during an interview.

posting: the act of copying files to a Web site and loading them onto the server. This enables the portfolios to be viewed on the Web.

PowerPoint: Microsoft's presentation software program. For more information, see www.microsoft.com.

practicing educator: one who currently serves in a position such as a teacher, a counselor, or an administrator.

reflection: captions or small statements and explanations used to give voice to the various artifacts collected in the portfolio (Barrett, 2000; Burke, 1997; Wolf & Dietz, 1998). There are four general types of portfolio reflections: goal statements, reflective statements, captions as statements, and assessment and evaluation statements. These reflections or statements are attached to each artifact, articulating what it is, why it is evidence, and what it is evidence of.

relational approach: interactive, supportive approach to human engagement.

relevancy: how the subject relates to people's lives (PATT, 2000).

revision: a modification of work that takes place through a process or review; editing and changing for the purpose of improvement.

rubric: a tool used in authentic assessment to assess or establish criteria that are complex and subjective. (Also called a "scoring guide.") It is designed to simulate real-life activity and show levels of performance on a standard or skill over a continuum, ranging from high or expert level of performance to low or ineffective level of performance. See Chapter 2.

scoring guide: a scoring guide (also called a "rubric") is a set of guidelines for giving scores to student work. A typical scoring guide states the assessment criteria, contains a scale, and helps the educator rate given work according to the scale (PATT, 2000).

scrapbook: a collection of artifacts that are compiled over time.

server: a computer that stores information for use on the Web or by other computers that are connected to it.

standards: a description of what students should understand or be able to do; standards may be listed or placed within categories (PATT, 2000).

standards-based reforms: educational reforms that have been prompted by assessment and accountability based on content and professional standards.

summative: the final stage or end result of a process. Very similar to the summary or events adding up to a whole; a final or overall evaluation or product.

thumb drives: *see* flash drives.

traditional exam: a method of examination that does not rely on authentic artifacts but on answering open-ended or multiple-choice questions about a specific topic to assess proficiency or competence.

URL: Universal Resource Locator. *Also see* Web address.

USB sticks: *see* flash drives

Web address: the URL of a Web site. It usually starts with "http://," which is the method of retrieval, then is followed by the type of page (i.e., "www"), and then the Internet domain name. An example would be http://www.microsoft.com or http://www.netscape.com.

Web browser: program used to view Web pages (i.e., Internet Explorer, Netscape Navigator, Safari).

Word: Microsoft's word processor software program. For more information see www.microsoft.com.

Zip disk: a large-capacity floppy disk (offered in sizes ranging from 100 to 750 megabytes) created by the Iomega company. A Zip drive must be used to read the Zip disk.

zoom: zooming in on a document is the same as magnifying the content. The opposite would be zooming out, which shrinks the content.

References

American School Counselor Association. (n.d.). *ASCA national model.* Retrieved from http://www.schoolcounselor.org/content.asp?pl=325&sl=134&contentid=134

Astin, A. (1993). *What matters in college: Four critical years revisited.* San Francisco: Jossey-Bass.

Barnes, P., Clark, P., & Thull, B. (2005). Web-based digital portfolios and counselor supervision. *Journal of Technology in Counseling, 3*(1). Retrieved May 2, 2005, from http://jtc.colstate.edu/Vo3-1/Barnes/Barnes.htm

Barnett, B. (1992). Using alternative assessment measures in educational leadership preparation programs: Educational platforms and portfolios. *Journal of Personnel Evaluation in Education, 6,* 141–151.

Barrett, H. (2000). *Electronic portfolios = multimedia development + portfolio development: The electronic portfolio development process.* Retrieved July 19, 2004, from http://electronicportfolios.org/portfolios/EPDevProcess.html

Barrett, H. (2001). *Electronic portfolios = multimedia development + portfolio development: The electronic portfolio development process.* Arlington Heights, IL: Skylight Training & Publishing.

Bartell, C., Kaye, C., & Morin, J. (1998, Winter). Guest editors' introduction: Teaching portfolios and teacher education. *Teacher Education Quarterly,* 5–8.

Barth, R. S. (1990). *Improving schools from within: Teachers, parents, and principals make a difference.* San Francisco: Jossey-Bass.

Barton, J., & Collins, A. (1997). *Portfolio assessment: A handbook for educators.* Menlo Park, CA: Addison-Wesley.

Bateson, D. (1994). Psychometric and philosophic problems in "authentic" assessment: Performance tasks and portfolios. *Alberta Journal of Educational Research, 40*(2), 233–245.

Bennett, C. K. (1994, Winter). Promoting teacher reflection through action research: What do teachers think? *Journal of Staff Development, 15*(1), 34–38.

Bloom B. S. (1956). *Taxonomy of educational objectives, handbook I: The cognitive domain.* New York: David McKay.

Brown, G., & Irby, B. J. (2000). *The career advancement portfolio* (2nd ed.). Thousand Oaks, CA: Corwin.

Brown, G., & Irby, B. J. (2001). *The principal portfolio* (2nd ed.). Thousand Oaks, CA: Corwin.

Burke, K. (1997). *Designing professional portfolios for change*. Thousand Oaks, CA: Corwin.

Burke, K., Fogarty, R., & Belgrad, S. (1994). *The mindful school: The portfolio connection*. Thousand Oaks, CA: Corwin.

Calhoun, E. F. (1994a). *Action research: Inquiry, reflection, and decision-making facilitators' guide*. Alexandria, VA: Association for Supervision and Curriculum Development.

Calhoun, E. F. (1994b). *How to use action research in the self-renewing school*. Alexandria, VA: Association for Supervision and Curriculum Development.

Campbell, C., & Dahir, C. (1997). *Sharing the vision: The National School Counseling Standards*. Alexandria, VA: American School Counseling Association Press.

Campbell, D. M., Cignetti, P. B., Melenyzer, B. J., Nettles, D. H., & Wyman, R. M., Jr. (2001). *How to develop a professional portfolio: A manual for teachers*. Boston: Allyn & Bacon.

Campbell, D. M., Cignetti, P. B., Melenyzer, B. J., Nettles, D. H., & Wyman, R. M., Jr. (2004). *How to develop a professional portfolio: A manual for teachers* (3rd ed.). Boston: Allyn & Bacon.

Campbell, D. M., Melenyzer, B. J., Nettles, D. H., & Wyman, R. M., Jr. (2000). *Portfolio and performance assessment in teacher education*. Boston: Allyn & Bacon.

Charles, C. M. (2005). *Building classroom discipline* (8th ed.). Boston: Allyn & Bacon.

Council of Chief State School Officers. (1996, November 2). *Interstate School Leaders Licensure Consortium standards for school leaders*. Retrieved July 19, 2004, from http://www.ccsso.org/projects/Interstate_School_Leaders_Licensure_Consortium/

Covey, S. (1990). *The 7 habits of highly effective people: Powerful lessons in personal change*. New York: Simon & Schuster.

Danielson, C., & Abrulyn, L. (1997). *An introduction to using portfolios in the classroom*. Alexandria, VA: Association for Supervision and Curriculum Development.

Dollase, R. H. (1996). The Vermont experiment in state mandated portfolio program approval. *Journal of Teacher Education, 47*(2), 85–98.

Doolittle, P. (1994). *Teacher portfolio assessment*. Washington, DC: ERIC Clearinghouse on Assessment and Evaluation, The Catholic University of America, Department of Education. (ERIC Document Reproduction Service No. ED385608)

Farr, R. (1991). *Portfolios: Assessment in language arts*. Bloomington: ERIC Clearinghouse on Reading and Communication Skills, Indiana University. (ERIC Document Reproduction Service No. ED334603)

Forgette-Giroux, R., & Simon, M. (2000). Organizational issues related to portfolio assessment implementation in the classroom. *Practical Assessment, Research & Evaluation, 7*(4). Retrieved July 19, 2004, from http://PAREonline.net/getvn.asp?v=7&n=4

Gathercoal, P., Love, D., Bryde, B., & McKean, G. (2002). On implementing Web-based electronic portfolios: A webfolio program lets instructors and students use the Web to improve teaching and learning. *Educause Quarterly, 2,* 29–37.

Gay, G. (2000). *Culturally responsive teaching: Theory, research, and practice.* New York: Teachers College Press.

Georgi, D., & Crowe, J. (1998, Winter). Digital portfolios: A confluence of portfolio assessment and technology. *Teacher Education Quarterly,* 73–84.

Gomez, E. (2000). *Assessment portfolios: Including English language learners in large-scale assessments.* Washington, DC: ERIC Clearinghouse on Languages and Linguistics. (ERIC Document Reproduction Service No. ED447725)

Goodrich, H. (1997). Understanding rubrics. *Educational Leadership, 54*(4), 14–17.

Grant, G., & Huebner, T. (1998, Winter). The portfolio question: A powerful synthesis of the personal and the professional. *Teacher Education Quarterly,* 33–43.

Hancock, C. (1994). *Alternative assessment and second language study: What and why.* Washington, DC: ERIC Clearinghouse on Languages and Linguistics. (ERIC Document Reproduction Service No. ED376695)

Hartnell-Young, E., & Morriss, M. (1999). *Digital professional portfolios for change.* Thousand Oaks, CA: Corwin.

Hebert, E. A. (2001). *The power of portfolios: What children can teach us about learning and assessment.* San Francisco: Jossey-Bass.

Holly, M., Arhar, J., & Kasten, W. (2005). *Action research for teachers: Traveling the yellow brick road* (2nd ed.). Upper Saddle River, NJ: Pearson.

Huffman, E. (1998). Authentic rubrics. *Art Education, 51*(1), 64–68.

Hurst, B., Wilson, C., & Cramer, G. (1998, April). Professional teaching portfolios: Tools for reflection, growth, and advancement. *Phi Delta Kappan,* 578–584.

Irvine, J. J. (1990). *Black students and school failure: Policies, practices, and prescriptions.* New York: Greenwood Press.

Jensen, K. (1995). Effective rubric design: Making the most of this powerful tool. *Science Teacher, 62*(5), 72–75.

Johnson, R. S. (2002). *Using data to close the achievement gap: How to measure equity in our schools.* Thousand Oaks, CA: Corwin.

Johnson, R. S., & Bush, V L. (2005). Leading the culturally responsive school. In F. English (Ed.), *Sage Handbook of Educational Leadership* (pp. 269–296). Thousand Oaks, CA: Sage.

Kerka, S. (1995). *Techniques for authentic assessment. Adult, career, and vocational education brief (ACVE).* Retrieved from http://www.cete.org/acve/docgen.asp?tbl+archieve&ID+A032

Krathwohl, D. R., Bloom, B. S., & Bertram, B. M. (1973). *Taxonomy of educational objectives: The classification of educational goals. Handbook II: Affective domain.* New York: David McKay.

Ladson-Billings, G. (1994). *The dreamkeepers: Successful teachers of African American children.* San Francisco: Jossey-Bass.

Landau, S. I., & Bogus, R. J. (1975). *The Doubleday dictionary for home, school, and office.* New York: Doubleday.

Lankes, A. (1995). *Electronic portfolios: A new idea in assessment.* Syracuse, NY: ERIC Clearinghouse on Information and Technology. (ERIC Document Reproduction Service No. ED390377)

Lazear, D. (1998). *The rubrics way: Using MI to assess understanding.* Tucson, AZ: Zephyr Press.

Lee, C. D. (1997). Bridging home and school literacies: A model of culturally responsive teaching. In J. Flood, S. B. Heath, & D. Lapp (Eds.), *A handbook for literacy educators: Research on teaching the communicative and visual arts* (pp. 330–341). New York: Macmillan.

Lindsey, R. B., Robins, K. N., & Terrell, R. D. (2005). *Cultural proficiency: A manual for school leaders* (2nd ed.). Thousand Oaks, CA: Corwin.

May, W. T. (1993, Winter). Teachers-as-researchers or action research: What is it and what good is it for art education? *Studies in Art Education, 34*(2), 114–126.

McGraw-Hill Higher Education. (2003). *Instructor's guide to FolioLive: Electronic portfolio tool.* Boston: Authors.

McKay, J. A. (1992, Winter). Professional development through action research. *Journal of Staff Development, 13*(1), 18–21.

McKinney, M. (1998, Winter). Preservice teachers' electronic portfolios: Integrating technology, self-assessment and reflection. *Teacher Education Quarterly,* 85–103.

McNiff, J. (2003). *Action research: Principles and practices* (3rd ed.). London: Routledge.

McNiff, J., & Whitehead, J. (2005). *Action research for teachers.* London: David Fulton.

Meadows, R. B., & Dyal, A. B. (1999, Winter). Implementing portfolio assessment in the development of school administrators: Improving preparation for educational leadership. *Education, 120*(2), 304–315.

Miller, D. M., & Pine, G. J. (1990, Summer). Advancing professional inquiry for educational improvement through action research. *Journal of Staff Development, 11*(3), 56–61.

Mills, G. E. (2003). *Action research: A guide for the teacher researcher.* Upper Saddle River, NJ: Merrill/Prentice Hall.

Morris, W. (Ed.). (1976). *The American Heritage dictionary.* Boston: Houghton Mifflin.

Murray, J. (1997). *Successful faculty development and evaluation: The complete teaching portfolio.* Washington, DC: ERIC Clearinghouse on Higher Education, George Washington University, Graduate School of Education and Human Development. (ERIC Document No. ED405759)

National Board for Professional Teaching Standards (NBPTS). (1999). *General information about the NBPTS standards.* Retrieved July 14, 2004, from http://www.nbpts.org/standards/stds.cfm

Newman, J. M. (2000, January). Action research: A brief overview [14 paragraphs]. *Forum Qualitative Sozialforschung / Forum: Qualitative Social Research* [online journal], *1*(1). Retrieved February 5, 2005, from http://qualitative-research.net/fqs

Pennsylvania Assessment Through Themes (PATT). (2000). *Portfolio implementation guide*. PDF document retrieved July 14, 2004, from www.pde.state.pa.us/fam_consumer/lib/fam_sonsumer/20/23/portig.pdf

Perrone, V. (1991). *A letter to teachers: Reflections on schooling and the art of teaching*. San Francisco: Jossey-Bass.

Popham, W. (1997). What's wrong and what's right with rubrics? *Educational Leadership, 55*(3), 72–75.

Reason, P., & Bradbury, H. (Eds.). (2004). *A handbook of action research: Participative inquiry and practice*. Thousand Oaks, CA: Sage.

Riding, P., Fowell, S., & Levy, P. (1995). An action research approach to curriculum development. *Information Research, 1*(1). Retrieved February 5, 2005, from http://InformationR.net/ir/1–1/paper2.html

Rieman, P. (2000). *Teaching portfolios: Presenting your professional best*. Boston: McGraw-Hill.

Robins, K. N., Lindsey, R. B., Lindsey, D., & Terrell, R. D. (2002). *Culturally proficient instruction: A guide for people who teach*. Thousand Oaks, CA: Corwin.

Sagor, R. (2003). *Action research guidebook: A four-step process for educators and school teams*. Thousand Oaks, CA: Sage.

Salzman, S. A., Denner, P. R., & Harris, L. B. (2002). *Teacher education outcomes measures: Special study survey*. Washington, DC: American Association of Colleges of Teacher Education.

Satterthwaite, F., & D'Orsi, G. (2003). *The career portfolio workbook: Using the newest tool in your job-hunting arsenal to impress employers and land a great job*. New York: McGraw-Hill.

Schmuck, R. (1997). *Practical action research for change*. Thousand Oaks, CA: Corwin.

Sewell, M., Marczak, M., & Horn, M. (2005). *The use of portfolio assessment in evaluation. Cyfernet Evaluation*. Tucson: University of Arizona. Retrieved July 14, 2004, from http://ag.arizona.edu/fcs/cyfernet/cyfar/Portfo~3.htm

Shade, B. J., Kelly, C., & Oberg, M. (2004). *Creating culturally responsive classrooms*. Washington, DC: American Psychological Association.

Shaklee, B. D., Barbour, N. E., Ambrose, R., & Hansford, S. J. (1997). *Designing and using portfolios*. Boston/New York: Allyn & Bacon.

Simpson E. J. (1972). *The classification of educational objectives in the psychomotor domain*. Washington, DC: Gryphon House.

Smith, M. K. (1996/2001). Action research. *The encyclopedia of informal education*. Retrieved February 7, 2005, from http://www.infed.org/research/b-actres.htm

Steele, C. (2002). Stereotype threat and student achievement. In T. Perry, C. Steele, & A. Hillard, III (Eds.), *Young, gifted and black: Promoting high achievement among African-American students* (pp. 109–130). Boston: Beacon Press.

Stone, B. (1998, Winter). Problems, pitfalls and benefits of portfolios. *Teacher Education Quarterly*, 105–114.

Stringer, E. (2004). *Action research in education.* Upper Saddle River, NJ: Pearson Education.

Taggart, G., Phifer, S., Nixon, J., & Wood, M. (Eds.). (1998). *Rubrics: A handbook for construction and use.* Lancaster, PA: Technomics.

Tannenbaum, J. (1996). *Practical ideas for alternative assessment for ESL students.* Washington, DC: ERIC Clearinghouse on Languages and Linguistics. (ERIC Document Reproduction Service No. ED395500)

Wiggins, G. (1999). *Educative assessment. Designing assessments to inform and improve student performance.* San Francisco: Jossey-Bass.

Wiggins, G., & McTighe, J. (2000). *Understanding by design* (Rev. ed.). Alexandria, VA: Association of Supervision and Curriculum Development.

Wilcox, B., & Tomei, L. (1999). *Professional portfolios for teachers.* Norwood, MA: Christopher-Gordon.

Wilkerson, J. R., & Lang, W. S. (2003, December 3). Portfolios, the Pied Piper of teacher certification assessments: Legal and psychometric issues. *Education Policy Analysis Archives, 11*(45). Retrieved March 25, 2004, from http://epaa.asu.edu/epaa/v11n45/

Winsor, P., & Ellefson, B. (1998, Winter). Professional portfolios in teacher education: An exploration of their value and potential. *Teacher Education Quarterly,* 68–81.

Wolf, K. (1999). *Leading the professional portfolio process for change.* Thousand Oaks, CA: Corwin.

Wolf, K., & Dietz, M. (1998, Winter). Teaching portfolios: Purposes and possibilities. *Teacher Education Quarterly,* 9–22.

Wright, V. H., Stallworth, B. J., & Ray, B. (2002). Challenges of electronic portfolios: Student perceptions and experiences. *Journal of Technology and Teacher Education, 10*(2), 49–61.

Wyatt, R. L., III, & Looper, S. (1999). *So you have to have a portfolio: A teacher's guide to preparation and presentation.* Thousand Oaks, CA: Corwin.

Zubizarreta, J. (1994, December). Teaching portfolios and the beginning teacher. *Phi Delta Kappan,* 129–136.

Index

About the Authors

Ruth S. Johnson is a professor emeritus at California State University, Los Angeles. She received her EdD from Rutgers University. She has served in a variety of educational settings in New Jersey and California. At the K–12 level, she has been a classroom teacher, an instructional consultant, a director of elementary education, an analyst, an assistant superintendent of schools in the areas of curriculum and business, and a superintendent of schools. She was a compensatory education consultant for the New Jersey Department of Education. Her major scholarly interests and publications focus on processes related to changing the academic culture of urban schools, with an emphasis on access and equity. Her second book, *Using Data to Close the Achievement Gap: Measuring Equity in Our Schools,* published in 2002, has been designated a bestseller by Corwin Press. In addition to her two published books, she has written numerous book chapters, articles, editorials, research reports, and manuscript reviews. As a recognized speaker, she has presented nationally to scholarly and professional audiences and serves as a consultant to schools and districts.

J. Sabrina Mims-Cox is currently professor of education at California State University, Los Angeles, and director of the Los Angeles Accelerated Schools Center. Her primary areas of research and interest include multilingual/multicultural education, emergent literacy, new models of teacher education in a global community, and school transformation. She has authored several children's reading textbook series in both Spanish and English, along with numerous articles in professional journals. She has presented internationally on the topics of school transformation and reform and serves as an educational consultant for a variety of organizations, including Rotary International, the International Reading Association, the American Egyptian Master Teacher Exchange Program, and Intel Teach to the Future.

Adelaide Doyle-Nichols is an associate professor in instructional technology, and instructional technology program coordinator, at California

State University, Los Angeles. Recognizing the need to integrate technology into the curriculum as a fundamental piece of teacher education, she enjoys teaching teachers to use technology in the classroom. Her primary areas of research and interest include technology integration in education, computer anxiety, distance education, and computer-based instruction.

All three authors have been actively engaged in portfolio development with teacher and administrator candidates at California State University, Los Angeles.